SOME DAYS

SOME DAYS

NOTES FROM THE HEART OF RECOVERY

BY THE AUTHOR OF
EACH DAY A NEW BEGINNING

1817

A Hazelden Book

Harper & Row, Publishers, San Francisco

New York, Grand Rapids, Philadelphia, St. Louis
London, Singapore, Sydney, Tokyo, Toronto

FIRST HARPER & ROW EDITION PUBLISHED IN 1990.

Library of Congress Cataloging-in-Publication Data

Author of Each day a new beginning.
    Some days : notes from the heart of recovery / by the author of Each day a new beginning.—1st Harper & Row ed.
      p. cm.
    "A Hazelden book."
    ISBN 0–06–255405–0
    1. Alcoholics—Rehabilitation.   I. Title.
HV5275.A98   1990
242'.643—dc20   90–4303
                                                  CIP

90 91 92 93 94 RINAM 10 9 8 7 6 5 4 3 2 1

This edition is printed on acid-free paper that meets the American National Standards Institute Z39.48 standard.

Introduction

For some time I've yearned to explore again some of the specifics of my journey—my journey as a woman recovering and my journey as detailed in the book of meditations I wrote a few years ago, *Each Day a New Beginning.* One of the real gifts of having written *Each Day* is the connection it gave me to so many women who, like me, are recovering in Alcoholics Anonymous or some other Twelve Step program. Many times in these last few years when I've been struggling, I have been strengthened just knowing that we are in each other's lives. It's been a comforting feeling knowing we've developed a relationship, even though we wouldn't recognize each other on the street. I don't for a minute doubt our spiritual connection with each other.

Recovery is a dynamic process, which means the principles or ideas that guide us take on new meaning as the days and years go by. While my voice is still that of *Each Day,* it has developed new inflections over the years. A lot was revealed in *Each Day* about the kind of program I've tried to work and the spiritual philosophy that has guided me. But there are many day-to-day struggles and conflicts that show different sides of me that can't be revealed in meditations. And this is what I want to share now. I want to connect again with recovering women—women growing and learning and changing and hoping.

While my emotional and spiritual well-being rely on being in healthy communion with others, my need to connect in a really profound way with my Higher Power is facilitated through my writing, a very solitary and isolating activity. But writing forces me to get quiet.

Then my inner voice, which I understand as God, can flow through me and on to my tablet. Writing becomes almost a conversation between my Higher Power and me. I know I'm not alone when I pick up my tablet and pen.

I want to be honest with you and reveal that I didn't know just where this body of writing would go. I had to trust that as long as I kept my ego out of the way, what evolved would be exactly what I needed. I hope that it will nurture or satisfy you in some measure as well.

The writings that follow at times reflect my adherence to the principles for living that I believe in, principles that I've adopted through years of vigilance to the AA program. And at other times they show how I get off course as I find ways to complicate my life. I know that how much I struggle on any given day is directly related to my distance from my Higher Power. When my Higher Power is the center of my life, I'm on course and quite happy, loving, and joyful, and assuredly fulfilling the role designed for me. But, like anyone's, mine is a program of progress, not perfection, and as these journal entries reveal, I stumble a lot. But I have never lost hope that I am on the right path.

I hope that what I've written will touch you in some important ways in your own recovery and inspire you to also write for yourself. I think that through writing we can find clarity whatever the situation, whether a problem is plaguing us, or is only nipping at our heels.

For many years I have kept journals. In fact, it was the act of journaling that inspired the collection of writings that came to be *Each Day a New Beginning.* I never knew when I was writing *Each Day* that it would have any real meaning for other women. More than anything, the book was a collection of meditations I was writing for myself as a way to find my own growth and particularly my own connection to my Higher Power. I was simply trying to sort out my life and find my growth and recovery. It wasn't until I had written the 366 meditations that I even dared share it with a publisher. It was only a silent, secret dream that it might sometime be published.

My own journaling formally began after the end of my first marriage. I was desperately seeking solace and security and went to a women's support group. The facilitator encouraged me to journal so I could gain objectivity about who I was, where I'd been, and where I wanted to go. It was an amazing, enlightening process for me. I was able to see how day after day I remained stuck because of my self-defeating thinking and behavior. Though it took a few years before I found recovery, journaling was a beginning for me—*the* beginning, in fact, of a tiny decision to *someday* change my life.

I taught creative writing for a while, and many of my students often talked about writer's block. Writer's block has never been a problem for me. As a young girl I was an avid writer and teller of stories. When I was an elementary school student, I used to create the basic story structure in my mind as I walked home from playing at a friend's house. When I'd get home, I'd promptly sit down and write these sad, melodramatic tales about what I anticipated would be my adult life. I lived in the fantasy world created by my vivid imagination.

Writing had empowered me as a child, and journaling empowered me as a young woman. I wanted to help my students find the joy from writing that I had found, and I remembered a story a priest friend had shared about nurturing the child within. I suggested they talk to the small child within them as a way of getting beyond their own block to writing. I suggested they go in search of a childhood picture, one taken when they were four or five. I told them to talk to the child in the picture about his or her feelings in regard to writing. "Let your child help you begin," I said. It worked. They loved it, and they wrote beautifully about the reconnection with their own inner child.

I took the advice I'd given to them and had my mother search through the bureau drawer where our old family pictures were. She sent me one taken when I was four or five. I haven't needed the child to help me write, but having her close at hand has helped me in many ways. For three or four years I clipped the photograph to my car visor. When I felt scared, on my way to work or in a gathering of strangers, I'd remember that it was my inner child who was scared and I'd talk to her, promising I'd watch out for her. In recent years I've kept the photograph in one of my meditation books. I want to keep her close and secure. Smiling back at her never fails to give me a sense of comfort.

I've used *Each Day a New Beginning* and made random selections from the text to bounce off as I get in touch with current thoughts and feelings. The dates of these selections from *Each Day* are listed in case you want to reread the earlier meditation or, like I've done, use it to check out where you are currently.

Secrets keep us stuck. I want to share my sense of who I've become and am becoming. I want others to know me, at least the me who has developed up to now. I hope to keep changing and growing and strengthening my recovery. Writing honestly helps me to see more clearly just where I am, just how I continue to stumble. It's this information that can propel me in new directions and toward healthier living.

SOME DAYS

It's comforting to be reminded that our lives are purposeful. What we are doing presently has an impact on many others. We are interdependent. No one of us is without a contribution to make.

—*April 9*

I remember reading Richard Bach's *Illusions* a dozen years ago—it gave me hope at a time when I was overcome with fear. On the back cover he reminds readers that if they are still alive, they haven't yet fulfilled their purpose. Simple words—but a message that helped to inch me forward in my early days. Now I seldom forget, as completely, that my presence is by design. Sometimes a reminder from a friend or a passage I'm reading will prompt my recall, but I no longer doubt the importance of my existence for very long at least.

Even when I'm feeling in touch with my Higher Power, I discover an additional measure of comfort knowing I matter to my friends and associates—that what I am offering to their outstretched hands and hearts is different from every other offering bestowed on them.

And I enjoy being the student to their many teachings. Even when my lesson is painful, as it has been these last few months with a particular friend, I know she and I both are gaining some necessary growth from this time of estrangement.

When I don't feel I matter, it's time to take stock of my many blessings—my good health, my strengths and numerous successes along with my yet unfulfilled dreams and goals—and forge ahead. The present calls us, *now,* and it's all we have, all we're certain of, and guaranteed to be just what we need.

5

Our dreams are like the rest areas on a cross-country trip. They refresh us, help us gauge the distance we've come, and give us a chance to consider our destination.

—*August 24*

My dreams from the time of early childhood have entitled me to attempt new activities, though often in secret. At age eight and nine I dreamed of writing about my life, I so loved biographies. And write I did—mysteries, love stories, and sad melodramatic tales—all extended and very secret fantasies of what my life might become. I composed many of my story outlines in song first, songs that I sang to myself daily as I walked home from my friend Barbara's house. My dream of writing never left me. During my first marriage I toyed with submitting stories to women's magazines. My first husband convinced me I had no talent for writing. Indeed, the subject matter has taken other forms over the years, but I'm grateful I didn't let him kill my desire to write.

I also dreamed of a career and independence while yet a schoolgirl. "I want to be a working woman," I said, "not a mother." But I certainly wasn't emotionally prepared for my many failed pregnancies. I remember proclaiming while yet a teenager, "I think I'll be an alcoholic," because I thought that meant fun, sophisticated drinking any day that I wanted. That's how it looked in the Doris Day movies I loved.

It startles me when I acknowledge how many of my earlier "dreams" have become realities. I've wondered many times if my *inner* self always determines my direction even when it seems off course. And who directs the inner self? Is it always my Higher Power? It has always seemed paradoxical to work on developing a strong identity that must become an ego that must be willing to surrender.

I know I'm not done dreaming yet. I hope never to be done. Although my dreams in earlier years often edged me toward unsafe cliffs, they also helped me soar beyond dangers. Dreams have led me to a good education, a wonderful second marriage, a strengthening bond with family, a strong recovery, a good job, and the completion of some books I've loved writing. In each instance my dreams led the way. I have learned that what we can imagine and hope for can be ours. A dream can become reality if we're willing to envision the steps we need to take—and then take them. I've visualized my path in detail and found the way as a result. Where are your dreams and visions taking you? Are you on a path that will fulfill you?

We will find serenity each time we willingly humble ourselves.

—*January 9*

It's easier to be humble when I'm feeling at peace with myself and God. The big ball of anxiety that used to live in my stomach, day in and day out, has moved on. My fears, most days, are minimal when compared to early recovery and all the years before that. But when they visit, my defenses emerge—and humility takes off with my peace of mind.

What triggers the fears? New faces, new situations, or old memories? Maybe all of them. But if I can remember to love everyone who enters my world, the fears will not emerge. Where there is love, fear cannot abide and I discover once again the fruits of peace. Today could have been more peaceful, but I let needless fears cloud my vision. Many days I can quite successfully and quietly let them go. Today I hung onto them, blew them out of proportion, and found little joy and no serenity. My day will be as I determine it, *every* time.

*Vulnerability is as much a part of being
human as is strength. Our vulnerability
prevents our strength from becoming hard,
brittle, self-serving.*

—*May 6*

Just moments ago I was in an argument with my husband. I felt discounted by his actions and words, and he felt likewise. I'm still trembling with rage and confusion. I want validation for my perception of our argument. I know my behavior and the resentment I'm feeling can only hurt me, and yet it's so hard to be vulnerable and try to mend our fences. But standing alone on my side of this barrier we've built with anger is not where I really want to be.

My shame and anger get so entwined. Acting strong and tough is lonely and dangerous for me. And I don't want to feel lonely; it's my choice to stay here or reach across the barrier.

Once again I'm wondering, *How did I get here?* Only hours ago I felt gently serene and quiet and close to my Higher Power and my husband. Now I feel terror. How quickly my rage came, how swiftly I closed the door to my Higher Power's presence. Will insanity forever be the distant cousin who pays unwanted, unexpected visits?

As close as our breath is the strength we
need to carry us through any troubled time.
—February 10

I believe this now, as much as I did when I first wrote
it, and yet it's far easier to believe in untroubled times.
My heart is struggling with this truth today. My last
twelve hours have been troubling, but I'm trying to
remember to "breathe in God." My friends at a meeting this morning helped me to breathe, and I came
home feeling saner and a bit more certain that God
didn't leave. And yet the terror, too, is only a breath
away. How quickly the change came.

My inner voice keeps whispering, *Forgive yourself for
yesterday's rage.* I know love is where peace and God
and well-being lie. Yesterday (a mere twenty-four hours
ago) I was filled with love for myself, for everyone I met.
I overflowed with gratitude. I was quietly at peace. I
hold onto the belief that I'll be there again. My shame
can only control me with my consent.

We need challenges in order to grow;
without growth we wither.

My challenges today and how I relate to them are different than a decade ago. "Not getting my own way" was a major challenge for much of my life. Working the program has changed all that. A challenge now sometimes means research is necessary. It might mean negotiations with another person are called for. Frequently it simply calls for nonresistance, walking away from a conflict to maintain my own peace of mind. I've gained my greatest growth from just such a response. My ego feels nurtured rather than diminished when I quietly, respectfully retreat.

Every relationship I have has been helped each time I've quietly negotiated or moved on. And I'm building a good track record that I wouldn't have believed possible a dozen years ago. Back then I fought everyone like a mad dog and felt justified. How tiring that was. And how exhilarating peaceful nonresistance proves to be.

We are just where we need to be today. The experiences that we meet are like points on the map of our journey.

—*November 9*

I'm comfortable with this thought today, but just thirty-six hours ago, I was far from content that I was just where I needed to be. Why the change? Today I'm calm and serene. I feel competent at work, and I'm not in conflict with my direction or my loved ones. It's easy to believe I'm where I need to be.

But when I'm scared and my turmoil is escalating and I can't think rationally, it's not with favor that I hear my sponsor say, "You're just where you need to be." How can I need that knot in my stomach or the trembling heart?

Deep within I know I'm safe and that my life is on course, unfolding opportunities to learn, to grow, and to share my talents. Wherever we are, and whatever we're experiencing, is only as disturbing as we let it be.

*Goals give direction to our lives.... Too
often we keep our sights on the goal's completion, rather than the process....*

For much of my life, I've sought acceptance through
achievements. I've wanted to stand out. As a young
woman, I tried to look and act different from my sisters. I succeeded, not to the pleasure of my parents.

But I also learned that positive attention could be
gained through earning good grades, working at an
after-school job, and completing a task I'd set for myself. And except for brief spells of apathy, I've been at-
tending to major goals of some import—a class, a
degree, a quilt, a book—throughout my adult life. Even
during the years of excessive alcohol and other drug
use, I was pursuing an education. My goals gave my
life meaning. Goals got me out of bed in the morning.
Yet much of the joy that might have been gained from
their "doing" was lost. My attention was on their
completion, not their doing.

I'm better at living in the here and now today, but
just this moment I had to bring my mind back to *this*
journal entry and away from that future moment when
my words are under your scrutiny.

We have been drawn together for purposes
wonderful but seldom readily apparent.
—*October 16*

I looked around tonight at a meeting and wondered,
*Can it really be true that we're gathered here by design, not
by accident?* Some in the group I don't really like. I question the honesty of one woman; another one tries my
patience because she's so negative and stuck on old behavior. For months she's sounded like a broken record.

Undoubtedly, I'm getting a lot of practice in looking
at my own judgmental behavior. My commitment to
love others unconditionally is not very solid, but what
better place to practice loving than in a setting that
doesn't elicit it easily.

Deep inside I do know my teachers are wherever I
am and my lessons are usually humbling. Am I willing to learn them?

Our prayers will be answered....And they will be answered at the right time, the right place, in the right way.

—April 24

As a kid I prayed a lot. In fifth grade I prayed that my friend Marsha would like me better than she liked Mary. In seventh grade I prayed that Dick would want me for a girlfriend. (At my ten-year reunion in 1967, I learned that Dick had *literally* died in the gutter of alcoholism.) In high school I prayed that Steve would someday marry me. And then I quit praying to God. I thought I had grown beyond God and figured *I* could make things work out through my own actions. My problems escalated and I prayed for change, but not to the God I believe in today.

I wanted resolutions to the many problems in my personal life, but the resolutions I'd hoped for were so wrong. I wanted my first husband gone—but not with another woman. After he was gone, I wanted marriage again and again with sick and even dangerous men. In fact, had I received the answers I so desperately hoped for more than a dozen years ago, I'd not be sitting here now, treasuring my life—I'd be dead.

God had a better idea. And the better idea was beginning recovery, returning to my family, making program friends, and developing a spiritual path. I'm now convinced that there is a plan for my life and that God will answer my prayers according to this plan.

Recalling how it was for me before recovery makes me shudder. I went from bar to bar, man to man, drug to drug—always looking for security. And nearly finding death, many times over. God answered my search for security, but not then. And not in the way I had counted on.

It's good to remember how it was because it makes how it is today so much sweeter. I don't doubt God's caring guidance today. I know it was there all along; I was simply too sick to feel it.

The awful memories haunt me, but where I am today brings a smile to my face. Even the days that don't follow *my* plan are part of *the* plan. It's a relief not to feel I have to be in charge of the world, mine or anyone else's. But will I remember this if next week is rocky?

.

Our attitudes shape our world....

I remember the first time I read the adage attributed to Abe Lincoln, "We're just as happy as we make up our minds to be." My cynicism balked, of course. *What pap*, I thought. And now I love that little adage. I believe it wholeheartedly too! And yet too often I resist letting it guide me.

When I'm edgy, like I was occasionally at work today, I don't quickly grasp how my attitude is muddying the waters around me. Hindsight makes it all so clear. Too bad my hindsight comes here at home tonight, not while I'm in the midst of "the mud."

In most instances, my attitude was pretty good today. I felt friendly and confident. Tomorrow is a big day. I'm organizing a gathering of co-workers, and it will be as smooth and as productive as my attitude will foster. It's a good feeling knowing I can choose my attitude and that it enhances or muddies a situation. The decision to "be as happy as I make up my mind to be" is mine.

It feels good when I accept responsibility for my attitude and behavior. Playing the victim of my emotions gets me nowhere—ever. I'm not perfect, but I can be in charge of how I act and react.

Taking the time, daily, to recognize the spiritual force in everyone and everything that is all about us, encourages us to feel humble, to feel awe.

—*May 28*

Repeatedly today I ever so quietly bristled at the comments and questions addressed to me by co-workers. Only rarely did I pause and remember our spiritual connection. When in conflict, even mild conflict, my ego drowns out the voices of our spirit. Fortunately my voice got a chance to sing after I came home from work. When I sat across from my husband at dinner, I felt the gratitude I'd been denying all day.

I believe we are all connected by the same spiritual force. I believe that my inner voice is trying to hear the message from the inner voices of others. When my ego gets quiet, I come to know other people in a special way. Why is it so hard to stifle my ego's screams some days? And why is it so easy other days? I'm certain it isn't connected to the particulars of the moment. Rather, my attitude determines what I hear or see in a situation. I can have a smooth day and recognize the spirit that is everywhere, if that's my choice. I don't think I made my best effort today and that bothers me. Thank God it bothers me.

We are guaranteed experiences that are absolutely right for us today. We are progressing on schedule.

—*December 6*

At my meeting this morning, I heard one person after another talk about their current struggles in recovery. We all seem to agree, though sometimes grudgingly, that our egos—which are determined to control the uncontrollable—are the culprits.

I'm so relieved when I remember that the size of my struggle over any situation is in proportion to the size of my controlling, inflated ego at the time. And though each experience is offered as my next lesson, no experience is designed to trip me up. Instead, each is an opportunity to inch a little further down this road to better understanding.

Life is easy when the turmoil is absent as it has been for me these last few weeks. But I need to recognize that turmoil is only there when I complicate my experiences by resisting them. Sometimes it's my perspective, bolstered by a self-centered attitude, that leads me to resist experiences. I complicate my life with such apparent relish some days. I can take a minor incident at work or at home and turn it into a major war.

I'm grateful that I'm at peace today. I can choose to feel peaceful tomorrow too. The experiences coming my way aren't designed to disturb my peace. And the real lesson is that my peacefulness becomes more of a way of life each time I trust God.

*Our fear comes from not trusting in
the power greater than ourselves to provide
the direction we need, to make known the
solution.*

—April 4

It's not very often that I now experience the terror that used to haunt me. Alcohol muffled my terrified screams before AA. When I was first sober, I tried to deny or swallow my terror. Sometimes I even fantasized about suicide as an "easy" release.

These days my terror is seldom spelled with a capital T, and that's progress. But on occasion it grabs me as it did a few weeks ago. My husband and I were returning from a weekend trip, and we got into a power struggle. For part of an evening I was sure my marriage was over. I thankfully had had enough practice with program tools to lessen the terror by remembering and trusting God. And the result was that both of us could finally see that our "not-so-recovering egos" were making us crazy. I'm so grateful to remember God.

When I move too fast through the day, particularly at work, I can easily begin to harbor a pocket of anxiety. I forget to let my Higher Power share my responsibilities. I simply don't have to do my job alone!

I heard at a seminar years ago that taking a fifteen-second pause before reacting to a crisis in the workplace brings a more productive solution. I've learned many times over that in any situation taking even a five-second pause and remembering God is a guarantee that my sanity will return. But sometimes I seem to have amnesia. I don't remember to remember my Higher Power.

Someone will be helped today by our kindness.

—*April 12*

It's miraculous how my bitterness or self-pity dissipates when I get outside of myself and express even a tiny bit of kindness toward someone. Something as simple as a smile at a stranger in a grocery store has changed my day. The reality is that the person helped by my kindness is me!

The rewards of even such tiny acts as a nod of acknowledgment or a sincere, "It's nice to see you," are momentous. Yesterday at work I experienced many such rewards. I laughed with my co-workers. I gave special attention to their concerns. I forgot myself long enough to truly pay attention to them, and I felt wonderful, even bubbly, inside. It seemed I floated through the day.

I'm genuinely helped by any kindness I offer. I have a dear friend who makes everyone feel wonderful when they're with her, and it's because she is kind—joyfully, sincerely kind. But it's so easy for me to be self-centered. And when I am, I suffer more than those whom I ignore. I know that expressing kindness prevents isolation, which is death to the spirit. It's really not that hard to be kind.

Our values define who we are. . . . Living in concert with our values brings peace to our souls.

—March 19

Like others, I value honesty, vulnerability, and expressions of love and openness. Hard work that is productive is important to me, too, along with a healthy diet and exercise. But treating others in ways I'd like to experience is probably my most cherished value—and the one I fail to live up to most often.

How many times a day do I respond to a question with an edge to my tone? How frequently do I brush by people, neither smiling nor acknowledging their presence? How often do I interrupt when someone is talking, sure that I know the right answer before I've heard the full question?

I'm not unmindful of my behavior. In fact, I often quietly wince at my reaction before charging ahead, not openly acknowledging my behavior for the moment but vowing to be more attentive, more respectful, more loving in my next personal encounter. And I fail again.

All I need to do is slow down enough to think and feel before I respond, verbally or physically, to the people and situations inviting my attention. I believe in the spiritual principle that all encounters, no matter how large or insignificant, are by design. My Higher Power presents me with hundreds of opportunities every day to practice living according to my values. Each time I do, I feel uplifted and secure. Each time I don't, my life feels unmanageable, and I hate the chaos I feel inside. But today was not as chaotic as many days are.

Forgiveness fosters humility. . . . Forgiveness should be an ongoing process. . . . It can free us. It will change our perceptions of life's events. . . .

—December 10

I remember so well a sponsor's suggestion years ago to forgive my first husband and pray for him. I was furious; after all, I had been wronged. And for years I harbored resentments toward my family, which only heightened the wall between us. Forgiveness, in my view, meant letting someone who had hurt me off the hook and never getting the apology that person owed me. This didn't balance the books as far as I could see.

How and where did it all begin to change? I can't even remember, but I do know that when I've forgiven others and myself, serenity is easier to experience. Feeling forgiveness softens my attitude and enhances the love I feel in my life.

Fostering a forgiving heart brings powerful healing. I'm awed by the relationship I now have with my family. Forgiveness was the key. My relationship with my husband is solid and healthy because we don't carry grudges or keep score. The longer I'm committed to the principles of this program, the more certain I am that forgiveness of myself and others is what opens the door to growth.

Our lives in all aspects are a journey toward a destination, one fitting to our purpose, our special gifts, our particular needs as women.

—*November 9*

I'm comforted each moment I remember that God is in control of my life, that my talents are God-given, and that I'm fulfilling some purpose. Not so very many years ago, I'd have scoffed at such an idea. I didn't believe in God, and I was certain I could control my destiny. And then my life crumbled at my feet.

So many days I'm helped through a confusing or tense situation by recalling the role my Higher Power has played already and will continue to play if I quiet my mind and stop trying to control. The journey has been determined and my well-being is assured.

I hope I can remember all of this tomorrow in the midst of a meeting I have to attend at work. It's a meeting that I have anxiety about because I want a particular result. I feel so crazy to be worrying when I really believe that God will take over the outcome. If only I can be at peace and reflect my values, I'll not interfere with God's process. I've tried affirmations along with prayer many times and it's helped. For me, any meditation technique—for instance, affirmations, visualization, or breathing exercises—can be a form of prayer. I think I'll work on breathing in God, breathing out worry tonight and tomorrow—even in the meeting if necessary. I know this works. I just must remember my part. I sure do forget my role sometimes.

The more we are in concert with God, the greater will be our pleasures in life.

—*May 23*

I'm basking in happiness and gratitude tonight because I was a speaker at a program for recovering people, and it was filled with love. The affirmations we give each other through our honesty push and pull us along. The butterflies I felt in my stomach for a brief moment as I stood at the podium were given flight by the warmth that radiated from the audience of men and women who share my journey.

How lucky I feel at this moment to have found the program. Even though it sounds trite, I can't begin to adequately express my gratitude. I can only look around me and marvel at all my blessings since God became my partner. This didn't happen overnight. Now here I am today, more content than I'd ever believed possible. There is only God's will and all is well. I know that now, but will I act accordingly when all hell breaks loose, perhaps tomorrow, perhaps next week? I hope so.

When we don't take life slowly, piece by piece, we avoid the greatest discovery of all, the person within.

All there is, is now. When I'm in a rush, which is too often the case, I am distant from me, the moment, and the special people whom God intends for me to know and cherish.

There is no real joy in the rush. The events are merged, one into another. The details designed to color my life hover on the edge of my memory, indistinct, ignored. Did I enjoy what I just experienced? Frequently I'm not even certain I was there.

Sometimes my busy body is only outdone by my even busier mind, and there is no peace. I can create peace, though. All it takes is a small reminder to quiet myself. Then I find me, and you, and the gifts that were always there waiting for me.

I enjoy being quiet, now that I've learned I can do it. I just wish I'd consciously do this more often. The days and weeks and years are slipping by, and still too often I am inattentive to what's going on around me and within.

I gave a good friend a five-year Al-Anon medallion a couple weeks ago. I was truly astonished that we'd been in each other's life for five years. The time had slipped by so quickly I'd hardly noticed it. I really don't want the next five to go so unnoticed.

27

The dilemma for many of us for so long was the fear we couldn't change. But we can.

—May 22

For decades I was certain the knot in my stomach was permanent. In grade school I spent much of every Sunday on the couch tortured with a stomachache because Monday was too quickly approaching, and I feared I would not read well enough or not understand the arithmetic or not be able to spell all the words. I also feared getting singled out by teachers who compared me to my older sisters. I got more comfortable with school and my studies as the years passed, but the anxiety I harbored in my stomach became a permanent resident. I was anxious about everything.

Through school, through my first marriage, even through the early years of recovery, I waited for the doom that hovered around my mind to fully descend. I became uncomfortably accustomed to my fears. I feared the present as well as the future.

Now the doom has dissipated. I'm not aware how or when the change came. Probably no one thing brought it about, but I know my reliance on a Higher Power has been the major thread weaving together my new outlook. I feel different. It's subtle but powerful. Momentary situations might trick me into the old, familiar grip of anxiety, but not for long. All I have to do is quietly remember that God's will is present; I'll know it just as quickly as I let go of my fear.

We can change. The ego fights it, but freedom from an old response is just a quiet prayer away.

Anger is an emotion. Not a bad one, nor a good one. . . .Our emotions reveal the many faces of our soul. . . .When we deny [anger], it doesn't disappear.

—*November 10*

I used to hate my anger because I didn't know how to handle it. Exploding at my parents or at my husband brought only short-term relief and long-term shame. Not exploding turned my anger to an inner rage that terrified me.

I'm greatly relieved that I get less angry now. Occasionally my anger rises as it did a few weeks ago, in full measure. And I felt *on the verge of violence* toward the best friend I've got, my husband. I still feel shame at how crazy I got.

My anger now is usually more disappointment than rage. But I don't pretend it's not there. Nor do I have to confront who or what made me angry. I only have to own it and let it pass. I've come to see that it's almost always because someone or something is not in my control. Coming closer to believing that we each have our own path to follow eases my need to control, which, thankfully, eases my need to get angry. But I still have a long way to go, and every day is an opportunity to make progress.

Gratitude for what's been offered us in our lives softens the harsh attitudes we occasionally harbor.

—*August 8*

I'm out of step with gratitude today, and I'm not fully enjoying any experience. I've overscheduled the weekend, and now I'm running from one meeting to another, to a baby shower, to a grocery store, and finally to dinner with these few moments in between. As I look back over these last eight hours, I missed the joy of the experience because I was preoccupied with where I needed to be next.

When I get on this treadmill, I have an edge that is evident in my tone of voice, and my sense of humor is gone. Not much about me is very pleasing when I've boarded the treadmill; my contacts with people throughout the day suffer and so do I.

It's so hard to balance the activities I want in my life and still take care of myself. To be fully present every moment when I'm with others takes a peaceful mind, and peace eludes me when I'm in overdrive, as I've been all day.

It is nurturing to be sitting here now, sorting out my feelings and reconnecting with my quiet inner self. Slowing down, even for a few moments, allows me to remember God; that's healing to my hurried soul. My life is filled with gifts for which I'm grateful, but I can't remember this when I'm not quiet and contemplative as I am now. Why do I take on so much when real joy comes in my quiet moments and my slow times with family and friends?

No circumstance demands suffering.
—November 14

I wanted to say this to a woman at an A.A. meeting today but feared I'd offend her. I sometimes wonder if I've become too naive or too shallow or too into denial, but I believe that no experience has to devastate us. We heighten or lessen our own suffering by choice.

That seems like a harsh response to give to a friend who is feeling that life is dealing her one rotten blow after another. But I believe that when we see the glass as half-empty, not half-full, the situation gets even bleaker.

I used to exaggerate the negative thread of many experiences in my life. My husband would say, "You can see this differently if you want to." And I'd explode! *He just wasn't sensitive to the seriousness of this situation,* I'd think.

Finally, I tired of being upset. I began to see more clearly how my own attitude played a large part in defining every experience for me. I had always known this was true, but I just wasn't very good at acting on it. More often than we like to admit, it isn't life that deals us rotten hands—it is we who shuffle the cards and arrange them in our hand to our liking. Whether we win a trick or lose it is because of how we play the cards.

I need to remember that my friend hasn't yet gained that clarity, and she needs my prayers, my love, and my compassion, not my judgment.

How common for us to look into the faces of our friends and lovers in search of affirmation and love.

—February 27

The fear that others didn't love me, didn't want to be with me, and didn't think I was interesting haunted me from childhood into adulthood. If my mother or dad frowned at me, I was sure I was awful. If teachers ignored me, I was sure they were comparing me to my sisters. If my first husband looked longingly at another woman, I was certain my days as his wife were numbered. I only knew who I was in relation to how others responded to me. I gave everyone important to me full control over how I felt about myself. I sometimes even gave that control to strangers.

I can't put my finger on just when that began to change. I'm not certain if time in the program healed me or if my strengthened partnership with my Higher Power did it. I only know that I am free of the obsessive need to search others' faces for evidence of how I fare. No more important measure of growth has blessed my journey than this.

Close observation of children can help us.
See how complex we have made our lives!
—*October 22*

I envy how intently my little nephew looks at a picture book or moves one wooden block on top of or next to another. For that moment, nothing distracts him, including me—his mind is completely focused. When he's done, he looks up, smiles, and moves on to something new. Perhaps it's the family dog that gets his attention; then the picture book and blocks no longer hold interest for him. He's fully focused on the dog.

My mind seldom switches gears so easily. What I'm thinking about at any single moment is generally being crowded by earlier thoughts or by something that will happen later.

We cheat ourselves every minute that we're not fully attentive to what's going on in the present. When I go on vacation, I move through the days more like my nephew. And I feel centered, more loving, certainly not hurried or harried and, best of all, I experience longer spells of peace.

Looking for good in others is good for one's soul.

Sometimes it's awfully hard to find the good in others. Being critical is much easier: it certainly offers no challenge. Today I listened intently, for a while, to a fellow at a meeting as he droned on and on, way off course from what I considered to be the meeting's topic. I shut him out a few times and then noticed others smiling and nodding in agreement with him, enjoying what he had to say.

My first thought was, *Why give him encouragement? He'll just drone on some more.* But I was refusing to let his words and thus his good come through. I was forming a barrier between myself and the whole group! I felt cut off from all of them, even self-conscious. This was a good example of how my spirit suffers every time I turn away from another's attempt to make contact. I know this deep in my soul, but I continue to turn away.

The opposite is true too. My spirit wells up with joy every time I look for the value in someone who is sharing my path, however briefly. What I hope to remember is that all those who share my path, no matter how insignificant their roles appear at the time, are with me for my good as well as theirs. It may not be until the next day or next year that I am able to see this, but eventually the lesson becomes clear.

Our behavior does influence what another person carries away from our mutual experience.

—December 12

A co-worker recently told me that sometimes I'm too impassioned when I present my viewpoint or my solution to a problem at work. In the process, I lose support.

In the same way, in my youth I argued bitterly with my family about politics and turned them adamantly against my views.

I struggle, more successfully on some occasions than others, to quiet my ego. I'm seeing that I can develop new habits. I don't have to react or overreact to anybody or anything. My treasured affirmation, "There is only God's will," is indeed a godsend. Ever so subtly, it's changing my life, when I remember to rely on it.

Yesterday I was at a baby shower where I met a couple of women for the first time. I hadn't really wanted to go because I was so busy, so my attitude was a bit rough initially. But I consciously and gingerly put myself aside and engaged a woman I'd never met in a conversation about herself. I felt rewarded tenfold because it was a wonderful exchange.

Every time I focus with genuine interest on someone else, I feel fulfilled. And every time my attention affirms another's humanity, both of us are fulfilled.

We are all we need to be, right now.

—April 7

Unless my ego is quiet, I generally feel I'm not exciting or interesting or articulate enough. My gravest fear continues to be that I'm boring. Retreating to write, as I've done since childhood, has been my way to minimize this fear. My rationale: if I'm not with others, I can't bore them, and then they can't shun me or, even worse, leave me.

My head knows that I'm all I need to be, that I'm evolving, that I'm gifted in my way just as other people are. But my heart fears this just isn't so, particularly when I enter an unfamiliar environment. The five-year-old girl in me recoils when I have to interact with strangers.

And yet I do handle this fear, in fact overcome it completely, when I step outside of myself and make each new person the center of my attention. Again and again, this action has richly rewarded me. Perhaps the five-year-old child in me will always be my reminder of how far I've come and of how I need to be gentle and loving to myself.

Perhaps everyone else has a scared five-year-old inside of them too. I wonder if thinking about that as I enter a room of strangers will change how I see them in the future?

Envy eats at us; it interferes with all of our interactions.

—*November 18*

I hate feeling jealous of someone else's success, but, in the last three or four days, that feeling has surfaced again. I keep thinking I've finally put envy to bed, but then it taps me on the shoulder. Perhaps it's my smugness about "how I've grown" that beckons its repeated intrusion on my life.

I keep forgetting that another's success takes nothing from me. There's enough of everything to go around—enough love, enough success, enough recognition, enough material possessions. My scared ego needs frequent reminding that we are *all one;* that we are interconnected spirits, each contributing our particular talents to one another. Each of us *is* necessary to the whole.

It feels good to sit here quietly ruminating and writing about my jealousy. It removes part of my shame about it and gives me the opportunity once again to remember that we are each on a journey. Another woman's success does not hinder my own. Her purpose, thus her journey, is right for her. Mine is specifically designed for me. I know God would help me remember this if I'd stop long enough to listen to the reassurance that's always there only a thought away.

My obsession with the jealousy that I hate makes it loom even larger in my consciousness. Instead, I could think about God's guarantees to me. They are real and will bring me peace.

> *It is no accident that we have been drawn here together.*
>
> —*February 14*

I'm comforted when I remember this—particularly when I'm struggling to handle my anger or resentment toward some person I think is hindering my progress. I used to think people set out to cause me grief, that they even derived pleasure from it. My first Fourth Step was really my attempt to take everyone else's inventory. Although I gave up that idea years ago, I frequently forget that every person I meet is a teacher participating in my journey.

When I do pause long enough to remember that, I can quit feeling negative toward the person. But not always! I have an acquaintance whose very presence makes me bristle. I see her as pushy, disrespectful, and far too authoritative and controlling. And yet I know our paths have crossed for a purpose.

Is it that I see parts of myself in her—the parts I abhor about me? And is it that I want the attention she sometimes gets? I'm ashamed admitting I've not wanted her to get positive recognition. It takes nothing away from me when she gets it, but I see myself as less if I'm not gathering in all the positive strokes being handed out.

It's really hard to look at who I am in these tough situations because I fall far short of who I want to be. But the lesson is that I *am,* always, who I want to be; and I must take responsibility for becoming a more loving person if that's who I really want to be.

No other man or woman is in charge of my actions or reactions. Each person can only enhance my growth. Only I hinder it.

The secrets we keep, keep us from the health we deserve.

—April 10

I had a brief but wonderful talk with a friend at work today. It was affirming because we share so many values and we can be open and vulnerable, trusting that we're being heard without judgment. We have no secrets from each other—this makes every encounter rich and uplifting.

Secrets create barriers, and I want openness between me and those I really care about. But sometimes I sit on a thought or a feeling because I don't want to start an argument and suffer the reprisal. And I know others have wished they'd kept quiet rather than tell me something because I judged rather than listened.

Sometimes my secret is that I'm angry and I'm ashamed to admit it. Letting *any* secret fester is un-. healthy, but so is angrily dumping it on someone. Finding someone to share it with, not necessarily the one to whom it's directed, is all that's necessary.

I feel so good when I've shared my secrets without complicating my closest relationships. I want my husband and the other key people in my life to know me, and yet I can't expect they will always love hearing every secret I have. It might be good to keep Step Nine in mind, and not share the secret with someone who might be harmed by it. Just share it with someone!

We have to learn to look with loving appreciation into the soul of that person... who stands before us. We have to practice being concerned with their needs before our own....

With ease I look lovingly at some people in my life: my husband and my parents come quickly to mind. But this spiritual value means that I need to appreciate *all people.* I didn't practice this all that well today. In my earlier years I didn't practice it very well with anyone. Before recovery, my parents were at the top of my "judged" list, as were all my family members. In fact, most everyone in my life in my first thirty-six years were judged rather than appreciated.

I've made progress, but still I resist appreciating a few people who keep surfacing in my daily activities. It feels as if God is tapping me on the shoulder. Again and again I'm given the opportunity to see through someone's exterior to their inner light, yet I'll close my eyes to it. I know I'm the loser in these opportunities and I can make the decision to really see within anytime.

What changed how I saw my parents was finding out who they really are—what they really feel about themselves and their lives. It opened a floodgate of feelings, and my heart has never been the same.

I can take a similar approach with others. God keeps offering the opportunities. How I wish I could be sure I wouldn't back away. I act as though the decision to really get to know and appreciate others isn't mine. I sometimes don't do what's best for me and others. But I have made progress and I'm grateful for it.

*Our challenges are gifts. They mean we are
ready to move ahead....*

—August 21

My challenges feel so much smaller, so much more
manageable than in earlier years. I remember a sponsor telling me challenges were gifts. I wanted to scream
at her while, at the same time, I was relieved that something good could come from them.

Challenges have not disappeared from my life, and
I still get caught up in trying to willfully resolve them,
at least initially. But I do take them more in stride than
before recovery. Usually, I guess, I've quit living in a
perpetual state of fear, and I trust my Higher Power will
see me through whatever the situation. And every time
I've moved through a challenge, at work or with a significant person in my life, I've learned more about myself and grown in self-acceptance and confidence.

It's hard to say exactly how I've changed except that
I no longer feel like an empty shell. With every day
in recovery, with every experience, *particularly* the
hard ones, I feel more substantial, more fulfilled. Recovery has given me tools to meet challenges that used to
baffle me. I continue to mature as I grow more comfortable with "doing footwork and letting God determine the outcome."

Life's challenges now invite my full involvement, and
this keeps me connected to the present and to my
Higher Power.

We will come to understand the part a
difficult circumstance has played in our
lives.

I told my story the other night at a meeting in another state and once again was overwhelmed with gratitude for having had a chance to measure how far I've come. This roomful of strangers and I were quickly bonded because even though we'd never met, our struggles were similar. The circumstances differed, but the message hindsight had taught us was the same. There was a protecting Higher Power along the many steps, the many years, of our journeys and we were saved.

I used to look back at my very painful first marriage with both anger and sadness that my husband and I weren't able to understand or emotionally support each other. Now that I see those twelve years in light of the inevitable progression of my developing alcoholism and my eventual recovery, I feel gratitude for them and him.

I had never had a consistent value system. I had never seriously reflected on who *I* was, as opposed to who someone else wanted me to be. I had always tried to disappear into the woodwork, never looking at any aspect of my life except in terms of how I was affecting others. I always lived in dread.

Now, thankfully, life feels fresh and clean and safe. Today I understand my journey and feel that no difficulty can thwart me for long. I'm quite certain that I'll be prepared for passage through any circumstances that may arise in my life, as long as I understand they are part of God's plan for me.

Riding the waves of gratitude, I get comforting feelings about where I've been and where I'm going. I feel like a major disaster could occur today and I'd remain peaceful. (But I hope I don't have to find out.)

What outlook are we carrying forth into the day ahead?

—September 21

How many times must I remind myself that the hours lying before me will quite completely live up to my expectations? I remember reading a passage in a book some sixteen or eighteen years ago that has stuck with me ever since. Two men were walking along a busy New York street, and one man bought a newspaper from an exceedingly nasty vendor to whom he was very pleasant. His companion wondered why. His reply was, "Why should I let his meanness determine my day?"

A positive outlook is within my control every minute in spite of the behavior of other people, unexpected circumstances, or distressing news. I'm in charge of my behavior, my thoughts, and my feelings. The quality of what I experience with my husband, friends, and co-workers is largely up to me.

I'm quite awed by how peaceful and secure my outlook is since I've been affirming "there is only God's will." Although the change is subtle, it feels solid—for now.

Our values define who we are....They
quietly demand that we behave responsibly.
—March 19

One of my values is to genuinely acknowledge another's presence, to not discount or ignore someone who is trying to make contact with me. I didn't do this today and I feel ashamed. A fellow from my meeting this morning came up afterward to talk and I brushed him off. He's been depressed and really struggling with family issues for months, and I didn't want to listen anymore. I don't feel good that I just walked away, and yet I don't want to enable his self-pity. What I wish I'd done was lovingly told him how I really felt.

Sometimes I just don't want to listen to a friend drone on about how hard life is. With little compassion, I want to yell, "Life is what you make it!" Am I heartless, or is that tough love? I know that some people experience situations that are far more devastating than those I currently face. And yet I believe we see what we want to see. We can exaggerate the negatives in any experience. Or we can choose to see the miracles, oftentimes tiny, within even the most troubling experiences. Life is either one grievance after another or one miracle after another. I'm the one defining each experience and that's true for my friend as well. But the truth is I didn't behave responsibly toward him, and I don't feel good about it. In some measure I want to address this because he's a friend and I care about him, but I'm also concerned about my own growth. If I don't resolve this, I'll withdraw from him even more because of my shame.

Every human contact is a message from God.

—*November 2*

Far too often I'm too self-centered to remember that everyone I encounter is God-sent. I agree with this in principle, and I am quick to remind others of it, but in the midst of most exchanges with friends and strangers I forget, totally, that they are carrying God's message to me. My own inner dialogue drowns it out. After an encounter, I may come to understand its spiritual impact, but at the time I seldom do and this saddens me.

Hindsight makes my understanding of this principle easy with profoundly significant encounters—like years ago when I met at church a woman named Pat who then appeared at my door just as I was preparing to gas myself. Our first meeting was God-sent; her arrival at my door was God's intervention. But ordinary encounters are just as profound in my spiritual development. I want to really feel the God-center in everyone I meet.

Being disciplined about other changes I've wanted to make in life has worked. I believe that I can use this same tool and look for the inner light in others. I'll not see it every time because I'll not always remember to look, and my noisy mind will lead me astray too. But intention is half the struggle. And I know my vision of all aspects of my life can change if I adhere to this discipline. It's exhilarating just knowing that the power is within me to see what's truly *there* if I want to.

*What doesn't come our way today, will
come when the time is right.*

At least four or five people in my meeting today com-
plained that God's timetable is too slow. They needed
the job or the relationship now! It's been awhile since
I've struggled with God's timetable for me, but I really
want God's timing to speed up for some dear friends.
They are active alcoholics and I want them to get sober,
now! I have to remind myself over and over that they,
too, have Higher Powers and their time to get sober is
not in my control.

I do believe *there is a right time for everything.* It's comforting, in the midst of turmoil, to remember my past
and thus savor that thought. I know that my success
in my work is because I was in the right place at the
right time. But it was important that I willingly accepted
God's timetable.

We can always close the door on the opportunities
that God presents to us and thus thwart the timetable.
Fear leads us to do that sometimes. But we can trust
that what is right for us will come our way when the
time is right. We need have no fear.

When we look around us today, we know
that the persons in our midst need our best, ·
and they're not there by accident but by
Divine appointment.

I love knowing that my experiences are being orchestrated by a Divine plan. Nothing has the potential to sting very long when I remember that. The trauma of earlier, more painful times I now understand. Each experience and every person involved made their contributions to the Divine design for my life just as I contributed to theirs.

I have far fewer upheavals in my life now than before recovery or even in the earlier years of recovery. And I know that the people haven't become "easier to handle" and the experiences less traumatic. It's my perspective that has changed, and, with my Higher Power's help, I sometimes make pleasant music of experiences that I'd have turned into barroom brawls in earlier days.

I appreciated so few people who surrounded me in the first three decades of my life. With sobriety so much has changed. Many days I am overwhelmed with appreciation and glimpses of real understanding. I know, without question, that the lessons to come are carefully planned for my development. I'm given the opportunity to offer my best, and my wise inner Guide will continue to give me the strength and direction I need. The choice to heed it or not will always be mine. The stress in my life, when I don't heed my inner Guide, is of my own making.

I continue to struggle with this choice in regard to one woman in my life. My envy keeps stifling my growth and diminishing her value in my life, but I know that her presence is divinely inspired.

I keep affirming the feeling and response I want to have toward her. And I trust my attitude will change. Hindsight reminds me how often this has been true before.

I feel such shame because I'm not giving her my best. I seldom even Act As If. I do believe rich rewards await me when I genuinely appreciate her presence as divine and important to my growth.

What we each discover again and again, is
that the solution to any problem becomes
apparent when we stop searching for it.

—June 25

Having a quiet mind unravels my many troubled thoughts, but ironically that takes effort. It's far more natural for my mind, in its search for answers, to race from one cluttered sequence of thoughts to another, blocking out the answer or the direction I'm hoping for.

I used to think a quiet mind simply had to "happen" to me, as though I'd suddenly discover quietness and my life would never again be the same. Instead I've found it necessary to practice the technique of quieting my mind through suggestion. Sometimes I have to come back to the suggestion again and again because of the flurry of thoughts that fight for attention, but I've decided that's okay. I'm not a failure just because I need repeated practice.

Today I'm struggling to get quiet enough even to practice. I'm blue and discontent. I can't surface a feeling of gratitude or a whisper of enthusiasm. It's a day when I want to hide under the covers, but I won't. I fight the feelings rather than accept them so they can pass. My mind scavenges to attach meaning to the feelings rather than to quietly rest knowing that in God's world, and thus my world too, all is well.

How hard I make my blessed life some days. And why?

We have probably tried to buy happiness
with the purchase of a new dress, or shoes.
—*February 26*

For the past forty-eight hours I've been warding off
the desire to go shopping. I keep trying to convince
myself that I could really use a chestnut-colored skirt,
and yet I know I'm looking for a lift from my malaise.
Too frequently over the years I've rushed out to purchase fifteen minutes worth of happiness.

I'm isolating and my sudden depression thickens. I
know that getting outside of myself recharges my ener-
gies. Through the years, I've learned over and over that
bringing joy to others brings joy to myself. I am well
aware that I can control this sudden despairing attitude,
but I'm defiantly refusing to use the tools that will assure my freedom from it.

It's beautiful outside today: the sun is shining and
warm and here I sit refusing to even venture out. I'm
refusing to let the blessings of good health, a good job,
a good husband, and good friends bring a smile. I can
feel the tug to move deeper into this malaise, and I'm
frightened by that. I know I must get active. I must
make a move to break this downward spiral. I must
resist the temptation to descend.

Laughter came so easily a few days ago. Even Satur-
day morning at AA I said I was on "a roll" of good feelings, and, mysteriously, I've let them slip away.

I think it's time to remember, studiously if necessary,
that God didn't move away, I did, and that all is well
in my world if I believe it. The affirmation that has come
to mean so much to me lately, "There is only God's
will," can bring peace. It will relieve my discontent if

51

I'll quiet my mind and offer my love to someone in my path today.

Thankfully, I do know that this is the way my life will work best. But I have to take the necessary steps. I'm wavering and I'm angry that I'm wavering. I'm ashamed even. I've got such a good life and here I sit. For God's sake, lady, look around!

.

.

Our worries about the future are over, if we want them to be.

—September 26

For nearly four decades I was a constant worrier. As a child I worried whether Marsha or Mary or Barbara would wait for me after school. As I got older, I worried about my grades and whether Steve, my boyfriend, would continue to like me. I worried about getting a good job. I worried whether someone would choose me to marry. And in my first marriage, I feared abandonment.

A friend told me some years ago that my furrowed brow revealed my constant worry. By then I was so accustomed to worrying as a state of mind that I wasn't even aware it possessed me. I never expected to live differently. And then I found the program.

Worry is no longer my constant companion. At times, I'll experience *days* when it doesn't shadow my footsteps. But it can and does very easily dog my steps when I choose worry over my Higher Power as a companion. When I'm free of worry, it's due solely to my making the choice.

When I invite my Higher Power, as I consciously do each morning in prayer, to come to work with me, to go to meetings (particularly ones I expect will be tense), to resolve conflicts between my husband and me, to give me confidence and peace for the hours ahead, my worries take leave, at least for that time. When I remember the presence of my Higher Power, I am unable to fathom a reason for worry. I don't always remember, but I'm making progress. In this, my fifth decade, it's less often that my brow furrows and more often that

53

I feel peaceful. I need to remember when a tiny worry begins to tug at my mind that I've slipped away from my special Companion.

Laughter encourages wellness.

Driving down the freeway yesterday I noticed a sign in front of a manufacturing firm that said, "Try laughter. Its side effects are good for your health." The sign brought a smile, which I'm sure was its intent, and I thought about its value to every driver passing by.

One day this past week, the local newspaper carried an article about the benefits of laughter, and a wellness newsletter I subscribe to also praised its value in our lives. A good laugh changes how I see everything, particularly when I'm able to laugh at myself.

Last night my husband was goading me into laughing at myself; at first I vehemently resisted, storming at him instead. Then my resistance broke and I gave way to laughter. It felt so good, and it heightened my feeling of appreciation and love for him.

Our lives, alone and in relationship with others, are healed a bit with each small chuckle. Days when I don't find reason or time to laugh bring me little joy, which in turn means I bring little joy to others.

The older I get, the more aware I am of how quickly time is passing. I want to savor the moments more and enrich them with laughter.

I have a neighbor who laughs at nothing anymore. He's angry and hateful and experiences no joy in living. I can avoid that by not taking myself too seriously, by daring to laugh even when my false pride argues against it.

Every time I laugh with joy I feel in harmony with God and all the people around me, and I am at ease.

We learn who we really are by closely observing our behavior toward the people in our lives.

—January 11

In the last two days, I became quite aware, once again, that I am not living up to my own standards of behavior. I failed at being a good listener; I interrupted others at a gathering at work because I wanted to make my point; I was edgy, using that tone of voice that I hate when it's used toward me.

I do so want to be a loving, supportive, open, and humble woman. But it takes a more serious commitment to changing some of my day-to-day behavior if I want to live up to these hopes. I frequently move so fast through activities that I run roughshod over people who are in my path and I know it. I even know it at the very time I'm doing it, but that doesn't guarantee I'll slow down, taking the time I need to ensure my thoughtfulness. Today I feel really awful because my abruptness precipitated a co-worker's tears. Lots of other circumstances unrelated to me contributed to her upset, but my part was not minor and I'm ashamed.

I know I'll do what I've done frequently in the past, which is to go out of my way tomorrow to be warm, gentle, and very respectful. But that doesn't make up for the hurt I caused today. An amend is appropriate; so, too, is acting in more thoughtful and consistently respectful ways.

It's really quite easy to sit here and make an honest inventory of my harmful behavior. I don't even shy away from making the amend called for. But I am bothered that I can't be absolutely certain that I'll not be this way again tomorrow. How well I know that I'm responsible for every action and thought I have. And how well I know that I frequently don't pause long enough to think through a response before striking out at someone.

I don't want life to be a litany of amends.

Pleasure and pain share equally in the context of our lives.

—April 8

Looking at a picture of me at age five, tucked away in my tattered copy of *Each Day a New Beginning,* flooded me with memories. I'm smiling and looking quite content and well cared for. I can almost remember this very picture-taking setting. My folks had a friend who was a portrait photographer who took all of our pictures. He even took the pictures at my first wedding.

In the picture I'm wearing a white piqué sundress with a red piqué jacket. My smiling face is surrounded by the "finger curls" my mother styled for me on Saturdays. Anyone looking at this picture would assume I was experiencing a very happy childhood, but my recollections are more often sad ones rather than happy ones.

What I remember most is being afraid. I was afraid my family would abandon me. I dreamed, again and again, that I kept knocking on doors of houses that looked like mine, and my mother would answer but always said she didn't know me. I was afraid of school and afraid my girlfriends would desert me. I nervously studied for tests because my older sisters were so smart and I was afraid I'd look dumb in comparison—especially since they'd had many of the same teachers.

My memories are seldom of a child secure and content with no worries. And yet my smile in the picture looks very sincere. I'm really quite certain I experienced lots of pleasure as a child, even though the memories that have stuck are the painful ones.

The same has often been the case as an adult. I've

lingered over the pain, somehow assessing it as more real than the pleasurable times. But I'm beginning to see a change in me. The pain passes more quickly and the pleasure fills more spaces throughout the day than in earlier years. I'm pretty certain that what's really changed is my perspective.

The more I choose to believe that life is filled with many small or great pleasures, the more pleasure I can see. I used to think that pleasure and pain shared equally in the context of our lives. I now believe we control how much pleasure or pain we feel. The longer I'm sober, the more I opt for pleasure.

Our prayers will be answered, sometime, somewhere.

—*April 24*

.

Somebody suggested many years ago when I was fretting over how to pray that I think of God as my friend, talking over all my concerns just like I would with a favorite companion. And I've done that ever since. Every morning I talk to God about the people in my life, sharing my hopes for them. I ask for guidance, for them and me. I seldom pray for specifics.

For the last dozen years, I've prayed for knowledge of God's will and each day, now, I question my own direction and choices a little less. I'm more certain my choices are God's too. Subtly my life is changing. Most days I'm more calm and centered, and I believe that God has caringly taken charge of my life.

My earlier desperate prayers that I'd be able to trust God's presence in my life have been answered. But I am still quite able to create anxious havoc rather than enjoy the companionship I've been assured. Today I straddle the fence between calm trust and vulnerability because of my feelings of separateness from others.

With God along I know there is no separation between me and others. We are one in God. The self-consciousness I feel is from my own isolation. I'm grateful that most days these feelings go as quickly as they come. Moving away from myself as the center of the universe brings a healthier perspective into focus.

We are each powerless over others, which
relieves us of a great burden.

I hate being accused of controlling behavior. I have always resented the accusation and usually deny it even when it's obvious I'm guilty. I react so strongly, no doubt, because I consider controlling a particularly reprehensible trait, even worse than jealousy, another old enemy.

In my saner moments, I am happy not to have the responsibility for someone else's behavior. The freedom it guarantees gives me hours and energy to spend in pursuits that promise true rewards. But I'm not always so willing to relinquish control, which is evidence that insanity still pays me visits.

I know I can't control traffic patterns or grocery store lines. I know I can't always make grumpy people smile. Still, all too often I believe that if I say just the right thing in the right way, I will get a co-worker or my husband or a friend to respond according to my plan. Thank God I'm not still trying to keep someone from drinking like I did for twelve years in my previous marriage. At least the controlling that trips me up now is on a much smaller scale. The hook, of course, is that once in a while someone does do just exactly as I planned, and I'm hard pressed not to think I've made it happen. Dear God, let me not forget the truth.

We learn who we are and who we can be-come through relationships.

—December 29

My husband and I are celebrating our wedding anniversary tomorrow, and today I'm relishing the gifts that have come from this relationship. We came together very early in our recoveries, and the road was rocky for a long time. What I painfully learned about myself very early in the relationship was that I still suffered severe codependency.

My first year of recovery I was celibate, socializing with women only. I felt healthy, so I was surprised when I did try an intimate relationship again that I was still haunted by fears of abandonment, just as I was in my earlier marriage, just as I was in my youth. Mistrust once again became my constant companion. Fortunately the program gave both of us the foundation and value system to grow individually and in relationship to one another. And over the years, I have "filled out," becoming more like the woman I fantasized becoming in my youth, minus the bombshell body and spectacular face, of course!

Could I have grown so fully in these many dimensions while not in a relationship? I'm inclined to think not. My experience has shown that the ugliness in ourselves can lie dormant when we're not in daily contact with an intimate partner. And it was that kind of ugliness that needed to emerge so I could free myself from its control. In the process, I was slowly and painstakingly becoming more my real self, a self still in process. I know that future changes will benefit us individually and together. The program has made it all possible.

Anguish comes of fear. And we so hope to avoid it. However, it seasons us as women; it enriches us even while it momentarily diminishes us.

—*February 24*

I'm really disturbed that an old fear I thought had been permanently put to rest is shadowing me again. But such is the case. My old abandonment fears have resurfaced. As a kid, abandonment dreams haunted me. Throughout my teens I clung to friends, both boyfriends and girlfriends, because I feared being rejected. In my first marriage and in most of my other relationships, I waited for and feared the abandonment I was sure would come.

In my present marriage, throughout the early years of mutual struggle, I fought off, not always successfully, the anguish of the fear of abandonment. It's nearly gone now. But when I'm feeling vulnerable or overtired, I look too hard for reassurance from my husband that "his destiny will forever be tied to mine." In the past few days I've had to specifically and consciously put my mind at rest with the reminder, "There is only God's will."

When I become fearful and clingy, he feels manipulated and wants distance, which naturally fuels my fears even more. The issue gets bigger and I lose perspective. Because my fears surfaced the eve of our wedding anniversary, they seemed hauntingly symbolic. And I'm very capable of overdramatizing just such a situation, getting further and further away from reality and my Higher Power.

What I'm doing to anesthetize my self-inflicted

wounds is frequently Acting As If I fully trust that God will care for me, assuring me that what I really need will always be provided. I'm reminding myself, methodically, that I'll never be abandoned by God, and my marriage will continue just as long as it figures into God's plan. What is right will endure.

I'm grateful that I've learned what tools to use to work through these fears, but I'm also grateful for the fears. They force me to go to God, which strengthens my trust, in time.

Our minds work powerfully for our good.
And just as powerfully to our detriment,
when fears intrude on all our thoughts.
—*September 27*

I'm feeling separate from the friends I'm usually closest to. And I'm self-consciously exaggerating my feelings rather than softly looking on them with love and offering sincere attention to their presence in my life at this moment. I've been here hundreds, probably thousands of times before, and I know without question the way to end my crazy feelings of separation. Sometimes, though, like now, I flirt with slipping into an even crazier realm.

My crazy thinking frightens me and attracts me simultaneously. I resist, at first, talking myself down from it. But as my husband and I shared dinner, I envisioned myself becoming hysterical, and I consciously reentered the sphere of the sane. Right now I have to be very deliberate in my connections to others—in conversation and in the quiet moments—in order to not pull back into myself where the unhealthy separation lies.

I am not separate from others spiritually, and in my saner moments I understand that profoundly. I need a double dose of this understanding today.

The spiritual wisdom that reaches me through the program, through what I'm drawn to in my readings, and through my intuition supports the idea that I am one with other people in God. The choice to see myself as separate, outside of the circle, is mine and I can reject it. It's too scary to stay in my delusion of separateness for very long.

*Today's experiences, in concert with yester-
day's and all that's gone before, are combin-
ing to weave an intricate life design,
unique, purposeful, and for our ultimate
good.*

—September 14

I'm continuing to struggle with my fears about the
future. I'm not sure why they have come up again. They
frequently come up when I'm going out of town, leav-
ing my "network" behind. As they have the other times,
I'm certain they will pass. When they come up, though,
I cling to my husband and my friends, and I try to resist
feeling vulnerable. I am ashamed of my fears because
it seems they are revealing to everyone my distance from
God. But God didn't move!

My husband is good at reminding me that I need to
turn only to God for security—not to my husband, my
job, or my friends. How painfully well I know this but
how angry his words make me. I always want the quick
fix I anticipate I will get from his hug and the words,
"I love you," even though I know by now that "fix" is
always short-lived.

I'll soon be thousands of miles from home, away from
my support system and the rituals that give my life
balance and meaning. I know I need to look within and
communicate with my Higher Power frequently. I also
must lovingly be involved with the people and events,
"the travelers" who share my path. We are not in each
other's world by accident.

We each have our destiny. I must keep this thought
with me and treasure it. Within it lies my security.

We are guaranteed experiences that are absolutely right for us today.

—*December 6*

I feel so much more grounded tonight than I've felt the last few days. And it's solely because of a program truth. I got outside of myself and focused on another woman who was struggling.

Here I sit, far from home, feeling scattered, self-consciously inadequate, and very codependent, and I meet up with a young woman from my home group outside of my hotel. I knew she was traveling in the area, but not that I'd see her. She was hurting, feeling lonely and confused. I played sponsor, telling her how it was for me, and I now feel gratefully connected to her. Again and again I learn that this kind of interaction is a guaranteed benefit to the sponsor.

I heard myself repeat all the program clichés that in my earliest days irked me, feeling their truth and profoundness anew tonight: There Are No Accidents; Keep It Simple; We Are All Teachers, We Are All Students; and so on. Throughout the evening hours of talk, I regained a healthier perspective on my own struggle. I've learned on many occasions how quickly it can slip away. And I've also learned the more quickly I turn my attention to someone else, the more quickly I return to my spiritual well-being. Tonight was a good reminder. We are our own students and our own teachers.

Through the discomfort comes the ease of understanding. The security that we long for, we discover has been ours all along.
—December 13

I miss my husband, my reassuring, familiar surroundings. I keep telling myself, *All is well,* but I feel lonely and doubtful. I've so easily quipped to a friend, "Each experience is just right for us at this moment," and now I struggle to make sense of my fears.

I'm questioning the value of my existence to those I've left behind. Do they miss me too? Or is it "out of sight, out of mind"?

Some of my fears can be traced back to a conversation with my husband the day I left regarding his future and his feeling that it has been on hold because of my job. I say I don't want to prevent him from doing whatever he needs to do for himself. In all honesty, I want to make certain what he does is compatible with my activities. I'm not letting God be in charge—of his destiny and my own. It's so easy to let God be in charge when that plan is consistent with *my* plan.

My trust in God's plan is marginal at best right now. I know I must surrender. The right outcome for us as individuals and as a couple is assured. I must use this time of turmoil to remember that God always has had my best interests at heart. And that will remain true tomorrow and tomorrow and tomorrow.

We must take responsibility for ourselves, for who we become, for how we live each day.

—March 7

It was rainy, dreary, and cold today. My coat didn't break the biting breeze well. When coupled with last night's fitful sleep, I expected to be a grouch throughout the day. But even the chills and headache that plagued me didn't prevent my better self from shining. I was very conscious of treating my companions respectfully.

We choose our attitude and our behavior and can respond positively to any circumstance. I'm mystified that I choose responsibly some days and not others. I love it when I determine that I will have a host of good experiences in the day lying before me. And I hate it when I choose, consciously sometimes, to court self-pity and harbor negative attitudes about the things I'm experiencing.

I see with such clarity some days. On those days I understand that taking things less seriously, deciding to see humor whenever possible, ensures that my day can be fulfilling and enlightening.

The external world does not control my internal persona without my assent. I have only me to praise or blame for who I am each day. Today I deserve a bit of praise.

What goes around, comes around....Goodness is...repaid....Life events do come full circle.

Sometimes I rebel against the notion that my destructive behavior will elicit a similar response from others, but it invariably does. Quite promptly, I might add. Fortunately the opposite is also true, and my concerted efforts at gentleness and good humor today resulted in nurturance from others. I needed this because I'm feeling lonely and overtired—a bit under the weather.

It's reassuring in a way that I get back just what I offer. The peaks and valleys are quite the result of my own perspective and actions. This affirms my strengths and invites me to behave thoughtfully and maturely. I'm only passing this way once, and I do want to leave a positive memory. The opportunities for this are myriad, and I hope I'll not duck them very often.

.

*We are never certain of the full importance
or the eventual impact of any single event
in our lives.*

—*October 7*

It's awe-inspiring to reflect on my past with a bit of understanding now. The chance meetings, a failed marriage and many bad relationships, some near-death experiences: all contributed to my unfolding character. The value of these experiences to my understanding of myself in the present is no longer in doubt for me. But I often lose sight of the fact that today's challenges and struggles will play a similar role in my future development in a way I may not know right now.

I have to be vigilant about staying in the present. I have to fight daydreaming even in the midst of important conversations. I struggle to focus, not on what others may be thinking of me, but on *them* or the circumstances that draw us together. I am making progress staying in the present, even though I have to give myself gentle, quiet reminders.

As I stay focused on the importance of each experience, I am more aware that an impromptu meeting such as I had today with two women who had come all the way from Germany was not just a coincidence. An encounter like this may be a key event in the unfolding of the lives of all involved. I do believe there are no accidents, nor are there mysteries that can't be solved if it's part of God's plan that the answer be revealed. The passage of time can clarify all events if I remain open to God's will. I'll discover, as I have so many times in the past, that my Higher Power has been taking care of my best interests all along, without my asking.

71

We need to make careful, thoughtful choices because they will further define our characters.

—*July 18*

I remember in my teens, my twenties, even into my thirties trying to "read" the beliefs and attitudes of my peers so I could demonstrate my agreement with their views. I wanted acceptance, and I figured that was assured if I shared all their opinions.

When my first husband would pose questions to me, I'd try to figure out what he thought so I could mimic that. I didn't know who I was or what I really thought. The first night I was alone for dinner after he'd left our marriage, I broke down in tears because I didn't know what to fix for dinner—I'd never taken notice of what *I* really liked. I'd always cooked whatever he wanted.

For the first thirty-five years of my life I had only the most shadowy self-definition. I became who I needed to be to fit quietly into the group. I was terrified of expressing a thought others might not agree with that I might have to defend. What a burden I carried for so long. How tiring it was to be on guard lest I not know the most acceptable response among the folks I was with at the time.

Freedom at last! It came slowly but surely through the process of my recovery. And the more I continue daily to consciously develop my views and share my opinions as these reflect *my* values, the more certain I am that my development as a whole, healthy woman continues.

It's like being on vacation to not have to second guess others! Even my periodic struggles with codependency and wanting others to like me doesn't weaken my resolve to adhere to my values. That's an incredible gift, one I cherish every day.

We need not wait for someone else's expression of love before giving it.

—October 9

Like a boomerang, love returns to me when I freely and honestly offer it to someone else. I didn't understand how this exchange worked until a few years ago.

As a child, I yearned for open expressions of love from my parents. The expressions were far less frequent than I wanted.

As a teenager and throughout my twenties, doe-eyed I waited to hear the words *I love you*, and yet was all but certain I wasn't very lovable. My offerings of love often came off as manipulative because I thought then that love meant to possess someone.

In early sobriety, I began showing my feelings of love to a few friends, still fearing they'd turn away. But they didn't. Much to my surprise, love was returned abundantly. I know now how love in its fullest sense can work, but on too many occasions I still hang back, waiting for my husband or a friend to show their love first. It doesn't always happen as I'd like. The pain I then feel is truly self-inflicted because if I share my love openly and sincerely, it *is* returned, if not in ways I predicted.

I'm still guilty of manipulative expressions of love, and they are generally not returned nor should they be. I must honestly take my inventory. Real love is never controlling. I know the difference well, and so do the significant people in my life. My authentic expressions of love allow me to *experience* love at the same time. Manipulative expressions do me and the other person an injustice.

My gift to myself is some time alone.
—*January 21*

I feel pretty crazy tonight and very short-tempered because of too many people around me. I don't recall needing solitude in my youth or even as a young woman, though I did spend a lot of time alone daydreaming. That was more because of my shyness, my awkward self-consciousness, not because *I* needed time alone to reflect.

Now, however, I need time alone every day, and when I'm unable to arrange for it, as happened this past week, I get rageful inside. I end up disliking people who are really dear to me. I get argumentative and refuse to listen. In general, I end up not being at all tolerant or likable and not liking myself either.

My current situation is further complicated because for the next couple of weeks circumstances will be much the same. I won't have much time alone, and I'll be in situations needing my full attention. Obviously, I must find a compromise or I'll lose touch with myself completely and create some enemies along the way.

I keep trying to focus on my good fortune, all that I have to be grateful for. I know that each experience is important to my development. But right now I don't care. I'm tired of people, tired of talk, tired of being on the go, tired of not having time alone to reflect, to talk to my Higher Power, to affirm my well-being.

My life feels ragged, not rich, and I'm resisting every positive message I've offered angry friends who've come to me for solace. I'm not willing to practice what I preach today!

I just want solitude.

No circumstance we find ourselves in is detrimental to our progress.

—September 12

I'm facing, more honestly, some basic aspects of my character on this trip. When I'm tired and have not taken time for myself—to think or daydream or pray—I become easily distracted, impatient, and irritable. And when I'm not showing respect and love to others, I'm not feeling it for myself.

I have made the last few days more difficult than they might have been if I'd taken the time to get a firm footing on this leg of my spiritual journey. I fully believe that this physical trip I'm on is part of my Higher Power's plan for me. It's unfortunate that I'm not fully appreciative or attentive to all the experiences. But I'm grateful to recognize what I'm doing. I know that's the first step to addressing the rest of the trip differently.

Each day offers new opportunities for a fresher, healthier perspective. I'm not controlled by what I did yesterday or even today. This gives me hope. Earlier today I was quite out of touch with hope. My chest was heavy, and I longed for quiet, home, and my husband. Now I feel able to continue this journey, knowing how necessary it is to nurture myself and take care of my spiritual needs in the day ahead.

I know I've realized all of this on other trips. Why must I keep relearning it?

Our struggles with other people always take their toll.…

—*October 10*

This meditation in *Each Day a New Beginning* speaks to me so fully right now. I have suffered an emotional relapse because of my struggle to control the uncontrollable: the events and the people throughout this trip. It mystifies me how my own spirit, so many years ago, knew the truth of this message, yet part of me still struggles to live in concert with it.

Deep within, we do always know what attitude or response is in our best interests. And yet my struggle throughout recovery has been between my inner spirit and my outer self. I know nonresistance assures a smooth outcome in any situation. And yet I don't adopt nonresistance easily.

I feel more aware today than before of how rich and peaceful my marriage is, even though we have occasional power struggles. I feel nurtured and invited to be myself. It's easy and quiet and peaceful in the spaces we share.

It hasn't always been this way. In earlier years most of our exchanges were struggles, first one of us controlling and then the other. But now we're generally at peace, and I long to see my husband, to share our quiet spaces once again.

I'm certain one of the triggers for my current emotional relapse is the contrast between my comforting home life and the present circumstances at work where I've created unnecessary tension. This, along with the intensity of activity and struggles for control, has worn me out. I feel very old today, but I'm so grateful to have realized anew how important intimacy and support is to my marriage.

Just as I've so glibly said again and again, each experience has something to teach us. And I've experienced, deeper than ever before, a measure of gratitude for the many soft, simple blessings in my life.

*Peace is assured when we anchor ourselves
to our God.*

—July 6

I'm more centered and peaceful tonight than I've been
for a few days. Nothing outside of me has changed, but
my inner voice has calmed me. I've finally taken time
to visit with my Higher Power and to listen. And I've
"spoken to" family and friends back home while
meditating, bringing them closer to me. The thousands
of miles that separate us seem not so far today. These
small rituals have brought contentment, and I believe
once again that all is well.

Getting off center, though painful for me these last
few days, has served a good purpose. I have defined
more clearly what I prefer doing with my time, and I
have become profoundly aware of what nurtures my
self-expression and brings comfort to my growing,
changing soul. I know far better than I did two weeks
ago who I am and where I want to go. Indeed, *all*
experiences are teaching us whatever is next on
our growth agenda. Our job is to be alert and willing students.

Real love is selfless love. It expects nothing
in return....It doesn't keep score.

—*November* 23

Throughout my childhood and even as an adult I've struggled with the fear that others didn't love me. Seldom did I agonize over whether I was offering them open, honest love. My focus was only on me and how they all were proving or disproving their love. I feared this would never change, that I would go through life feeling deprived of love, on the verge of abandonment. Never had I realized that love would no longer elude me if I gave it away to others.

I'm grateful I've come to understand this through the program and the friends I've made there. I believe that my relationship with my husband has been enhanced when I've been able to take the focus off myself and shower him with love just for the sake of doing it. I'm overcoming the old codependent urge to await his "repayment," and the miracle is that love does return tenfold when I least expect it—which makes it even more special.

In my youth I had no understanding of selfless love. Love was conditional and it was a trade-off. The scales needed constant balancing.

How freeing my current expressions of love are. The old way created burdens and tension, anger and defeat. Real love expressions bless and exhilarate, motivate and multiply. I'm quite convinced, naive though it sounds, that more frequent expressions of genuine love between all persons would profoundly change the balance of the universal powers.

Many years ago I learned "The Peace Song," which

expresses that peace begins with each of us. I believe this is true. I believe that peace and love are synonymous and each of us is charged with the responsibility of bringing the world into balance. We can make this happen through humble, everyday expressions of unselfish love to the people who just happen to be around us and to those dear in our lives. Because I'm an imperfect human, I don't always choose to share my love, and then my perception of the other person and myself is out of balance. What a pity. Life can be so much easier.

Life's eternal lesson is acceptance, and with it comes life's eternal blessings....

—August 20

I've noticed that I associate certain qualities to the way some words sound and feel as I form them with my mouth. Some words feel warm and loving, others harsh and cold. *Acceptance* is a warm word for me. My lips are drawn softly together when I say it. How I wish that meant it was an easy word to live more fully.

I speak so glibly about acceptance of the many conditions of my life that I can't control, about acceptance of others. When I am accepting, I am peaceful. But it eludes me often.

I've become aware that I go through phases where I am apt to be more accepting of circumstances that I don't like. When I'm with people who are overly critical of something, I will frequently become more accepting of it. I wonder if that's really acceptance or just my way to feel superior. At the time, it feels right not to join the criticism. This doesn't feel dishonest, though I know I am trying to separate myself from others who are complaining. I don't want to take on negative attitudes that aren't really mine. I have enough of my own! The paradox, of course, is that while I may be more accepting of what others are complaining about, I'm not accepting of the complainers. What results is, I'm still struggling with acceptance and am not very peaceful within.

And it's not just acceptance of others that troubles me. For example, I'm ashamed to admit how much I'm struggling to accept my body as I age. The world is full of people who are suffering with real problems, and

I am concerned about cellulite. My perspective is definitely skewed with unhealthy self-centeredness when it comes to body image.

My blessings go unnoticed when I'm in this frame of mind, and the peace that comes with acceptance is out of my grasp. I have the tools to change this perspective. I know my Higher Power is "in the wings" just waiting to remove this shortcoming; it's my willingness that seems to be a problem.

We can let our minds rest. We can give our thoughts to the wind, and serenity will find us.

—September 11

I sit here restfully today, mostly in solitude, and I can feel my psyche healing. Time away, time alone, time in reflection are more necessary to my mental and spiritual well-being than I've acknowledged on this trip. Or perhaps it's just easier to steal away by myself today than has been the case these last ten days because of the intense business we were conducting.

It's good to have these few hours alone in a quiet, restful apartment before joining my husband for the last leg of this long, busy trip. I especially appreciate that it's a friend's home, a new friend who has become very dear to me. I am old enough to be her mother, but we learn from one another as equals. While in her presence, I experience a quiet serenity, profound compassion, and a love for human life. She keeps giving of herself to me, expecting nothing in return, and I want to shower her with affection.

I think we will remain friends for many years to come, perhaps for more reasons than the ones that have already come to pass. I know, because I am able to trust that God is at work in this relationship, that she is not just a fleeting friend—and that brings me pleasure. Though I sometimes cling to people who don't offer this kind of deeper pleasure, I do it less as I get older and more secure. Treasuring and honoring people who are good for my life honors me as well.

We each have been blessed with unique qualities. . . .We each have special features that are projected in only one way, the way we alone project them.

I have just been talking to a very special friend about rejection and my fear of abandonment. What I failed to understand most of my life is that I am very special and need not expect rejection. I didn't know we all have special gifts that are just a bit different from everyone else's. I certainly didn't understand that I'd be drawn toward specific persons or situations that needed what I had to offer. I carried my fear of rejection on my face and in my demeanor. I think we often find just what we expect to find. As we think, so we are. To think, instead, that we are special and necessary in the lives of others diminishes not only our fears but the likelihood that we will be rejected.

In my spiritually connected moments, I'm at peace with this idea and have no fears for today or for tomorrow. But I'm not always in touch with my Higher Power and fears creep in. And then I feel very ordinary and rejectable.

At times like these my well-being depends on my positive self-talk or support from others. Most of the time I can get myself back on track, but I must take time to address my fears and smooth my feelings. I wonder sometimes if I will ever have enough security or trust in my Higher Power to have no more doubt. Perhaps not, but I do know that the less focus on me and the more on other people, the fewer my doubts.

Our need to be perfect will lessen with time.

—February 29

I must find, once again, the balance between too much and too little time for introspection and nurturing myself. Reacting perhaps to taking too little time for a few days, now I'm going to the other extreme, spending too much time being seriously introspective. I'm teetering on melancholy as a result. I need lots of laughter and play along with my quiet and serious moods to grow and heal as a recovering woman. But just as I did everything to extremes before getting into AA, I'm inclined, still, to extremes as I learn about recovery.

I must remember to aim for Progress, Not Perfection, and I have made progress. At least now I can recognize when I'm pushing too close to the edge of my well-being. At times it would be all too easy to step over the edge. It's almost as though I need this time of struggle back to my Higher Power and sanity. I think I test just to see if my Higher Power is really there. How crazy it seems to be saying this, and yet how true I know it to be.

It's humbling to get a little crazy sometimes.

That which we fear grows in proportion to
our obsession with it.

—February 20

Business travel is far more stressful for me than vacation travel. I worry too much that I'll miss connections or not be able to find my way around. I do not remember very well that my Higher Power is watching over me just as carefully at these times as when I'm in familiar territory feeling secure.

I don't like admitting my anxiety. But at least some anxiety shadows me much of the time. I say I don't doubt my Higher Power's presence, and hindsight clearly convinces me that I've never traveled alone. Yet I'm frequently not as free of tension as I would be if I were truly Letting Go and Letting God.

I'm eager to see my husband again. We've not seen each other for eleven days, and I have a slightly nervous stomach like a young schoolgirl waiting for her first date. I commonly feel this way when I've been away from him for a while. I have twinges of fear that his feelings for me will have changed. My rational self knows that's needless worry. I'm sure these feelings are rooted in my abandonment fears. Though I struggle to be free of them, once and for all, I might be better off holding them dear.

Some years ago a therapist suggested that the small child within is the home of our fears and that parenting that child would allow the fear to rest. I believe I'll quiet my mind, close my eyes, and hold my small child within during the rest of my ride to the airport.

*We are not offered a painless existence, but
we are offered opportunities for gathering
perspective from the painful moments.*

—November 3

I'm feeling grounded once again. I'm sitting in my
special chair with books at my side that offer me
daily guidance, my friends close at hand, and my
husband's intimacy only a quiet request away. After
many days of longing for these currents in my life, I
now feel at peace.

Perhaps it's age that has made me less adventurous.
I've certainly always claimed to love travel, particularly
to settings new to me in faraway places. But the quiet
and the familiar are what call to me now.

My sense of place and space has never felt more
powerful nor more positive. I like feeling rooted, and
even more I like admitting that I treasure the small
pleasures of my home, my study, my beat-up re-
clining chair that is a hand-me-down from my father-
in-law. I am not uncomfortable admitting I want and
need the stability of my relationship with my husband.
Nor do I shy away from my feelings toward my friends.
At home, with my husband and with my friends, I
know who I am, and I find welcome comfort in that.
Being hours and miles away doesn't mean I lose myself, really, because my Higher Power is always there,
and yet when I'm away—not here—I feel a sense of loss
that is haunting.

The blessing in this is that I've discovered once again
that my loved ones are not in my life by accident. They
deserve my loving acknowledgment of that. I thought-
lessly take them all for granted. And I take for granted,

too, that they'll always be here. As I write this, I'm reminded of a friend's very good friend who just died. My acknowledgment needs to be shown now.

.

.

I will take charge of my life today.

It's much too easy to slip into my old behavior where I was like a pingpong ball to everybody's paddle. Although I know I exaggerate this in recollection, for most of my first four decades, I was reacting to others rather than purposefully fulfilling my own role in life. I'm not sure I even knew it was up to me to define myself. Perhaps I thought it was easier to let others decide who I should be. I certainly don't recall struggling with identity issues back then. Not until I stumbled into AA did I grasp the idea that who I was was up to me.

My first moral inventory, superficial though it was, offered lots of clues as to who I was. I completed it feeling not at all certain I wanted the responsibility for my life. Blaming others for my misfortunes was easy.

The seduction to blame others still trips me up. Yet I only feel worthwhile and whole when I am consciously taking charge of my activities and my behavior.

Today was a good example of being comfortably in charge of me and yet not controlling of others. I remained calm, by choice, throughout the day, recalling with joy, whenever I felt the need, the image of my Higher Power sorting through each minor turbulence. That I consciously stayed in control of my behavior and attitude and asked for God's help kept the day flowing smoothly.

This is a lesson I wish I'd never forget, and yet I likely will. At least I no longer believe that God is keeping a big black grading book in heaven!

It's okay to want to feel good all the time.
                                                    —*February 6*

I know it's not realistic to expect to feel wonderful
every moment. Still, I harbor the notion that if I stay
connected to my Higher Power, I will always feel serene and joyful. Thus, I find fault with myself (all too
often) because I'm edgy, slightly depressed, or caught
up in the past or future. It is human to be genuinely
happy sometimes, but only *sometimes*.

I am happy more often than before recovery, and
more often than in my early recovery. My happiness
is the result of more trust in my Higher Power, more
trust in the process of change, more trust that "all things
pass" so difficult moments will too. But I also have more
reasonable expectations about what makes me happy.
No longer must a person or an experience be perfect
for me to feel joy. More often now I let each day's
rhythm fill me with an inner song.

Today was a good example of a boring day that still
offered moments of joy only because I allowed myself
to genuinely care about others. I know my happiness
is primarily my decision. Each experience is an opportunity for me to decide for or against being happy.

A friend shared a wonderful reminder at a recent
meeting. She said our only assignment in life is to listen
to and nurture our spirits. Getting quiet ensures that
my spirit and I will find peace and happiness.

It's spiritually moving to realize the truth of our authenticity.

—*November 13*

Only recently have I courted, and still not always with conviction, the belief that my contribution to the world is unique and important. I could generally understand this to be true of a few other select men and women I knew or observed from afar—but me? Hardly!

At a meeting today we discussed the Fourth Step and our continuing struggles with shortcomings. Occasional feelings of inadequacy shadowed us all. And I felt pain again, pain that I've felt often because I'm not as intelligent as I think I should be. I'm still smarting from the pain that surfaced briefly when I just couldn't keep up with the intellectual demands of a conversation. Among some friends, I once again felt like a phony—*How can I not follow this conversation?*

I've sometimes thought that God guided me through the schooling I needed to end up in my current job. And that, in fact, just may be the case. I do believe we are where we need to be—always. My job is really a small miracle that has come out of my recovery. I wish I could just hang on to the sweetness of this thought rather than the bitter, *I must be a phony.*

In my heart I know God's plan has a space for each of us. I'm in the right place for now, and I'll keep discovering it if I keep listening for guidance and trusting the outcome to God.

I feel better now that I've remembered, once again, how the program works.

*All that these moments offer will never pass
our way again.*

—May 10

My husband asked that I slow down tonight: I was
pumping questions at him, throwing supper together,
and providing a quick review of my day all at breakneck
speed, and I didn't even realize it. Only hours earlier
I'd mentioned to friends that I was feeling mellow, slow,
and deliberate and, in fact, was. Why did I jump on
the treadmill?

Actually, I think I've got it figured out. I knew that
I wanted to retreat to my study tonight to journal, and
I wanted some leisurely time to do so. I also wanted
to discuss with my husband a litany of things I'd jot-
ted down on my trip home so I could clear my mind
of extraneous matters and be free to write. In my rush
I failed to appreciate the quiet spaces, the times when
I could have simply felt the joy of living.

Hurrying—anytime, anywhere—severs my connection to God and the present. When I finally take note
of my "absence," I realize I have lost a few minutes or
hours of living. Times, places, events will never come
again in the same way. When I miss them, I miss rich
experiences that have been created for my benefit.

I cram too much into some evenings. And my discipline to accomplish what I'd planned on doing, along
with handling a few additional matters that surface
(which I hadn't counted on), brings the treadmill out
of the closet. I jump on board, racing to manage it all.
Seldom do I simply forego the agenda I've set for myself. Too often I'm driven to accomplish it all—and more.

I can apply these principles at work. What doesn't

get handled today will get handled tomorrow, and the consequences won't kill me. But to my personal agenda at home? No way! I need to slow down *here,* whether that means at work or at home, and smell the fragrance of the moment.

I'm a great vacationer. I never get overextended, and I do revel in the moment. What I seldom remember is that "vacation" is a state of mind I can recapture whenever I want to.

Claiming ourselves, the good and the bad, is healing.

—February 25

I haven't taken a formal Fourth or Fifth Step for a number of years. Sometimes I think I don't need one as long as I stay current with the Tenth Step and make amends when called for. At other times I wonder if I'm only rationalizing because I don't want to expend the energy. A friend shared with me today his recent experiences doing a formal Fourth Step, and I felt envious of his joy. I'm not feeling stuck or angry or complacent in my own program. But I'm not feeling the level of joy he radiated either.

In earlier days I had mood swings so often that frequent Fourth Steps helped center me. Now it's easier to skip over frequent check-ins with my sponsor because I'm seldom at either end of the spectrum. I'm at relative ease with my life now. But am I missing a level of serenity that only comes to those who stay close to their Higher Power through a humbling fearless and moral inventory? I need to meditate on this and follow the direction that will undoubtedly come.

I am quite certain that I'm glossing over some of my defects. Just because I'm not in pain or experiencing serious consequences as the result of my inattention to events in the present doesn't mean that I don't need to "clean house" and do a Fourth or Fifth Step.

My tolerance for mild discomfort regarding my behavior is quite high, and that's to my detriment. I honestly believe doing a formal Fourth and Fifth Step could help me, would, in fact, propel me forward and enhance my program. I'll do it.

It has been said that the most prayerful life is the one most actively lived.

—December 21

The depth of my involvement with people and my circumstances at any moment is directly proportional to how spirit-filled I feel. Getting outside of myself and attentive to others always, always elevates my mood and energizes my spirit. That I isolate and choose self-pity and self-centeredness is insanity, and yet that is my choice some days.

After reading *The Magical Mystical Bear* many years ago, my perspective began to change. For the first time I could see how much different I felt whenever I made a point of listening to and really seeing others instead of wondering, as I'd done for years, how they were seeing and thinking about me.

Actively living means being inside the fish bowl with others rather than outside, looking in. It means being vulnerable and painfully honest about myself and being willing to love, unconditionally, myself and everyone else. It means not sitting on the sidelines judging others but participating freely because this moment is passing, never to return.

Life is happening *now,* not this evening or next week or when I'm on vacation. Letting moments slip by un- noticed is ignoring a gift. I've been promised God's care and the perfect design for my life, but I have a part to play. When I'm uninvolved with the people and events around me, I'm standing in the way of the orderly out- come planned for my life and for the lives of those who journey with me. All I have to do is be alert and know that God is close by.

And yet my mind wanders, incessantly, and I struggle to keep it focused. I feel ashamed when I'm with a friend who is sharing something intimate and I realize I've mentally wandered away. I really want to change this behavior. I know I'm cheating myself, but there are times I feel powerless over my inattention.

.

Opportunities are offered when we are ready for them.

So many years ago my sponsor told me that God had my life in tow—that I was progressing according to my "chart." She insisted that *when the time was right* I'd find the perfect job and the perfect relationship. It took patience and lots of prayer to accept her wisdom. But before doing so I tried to force many unworkable situations. In retrospect, I am grateful God's way prevailed.

Now I try to share that wisdom with others. I've watched it work in countless lives, including my own. And still, much too often, I forget and try to force a situation or waste God's time and my own praying for a change in someone else's life.

How can I know something so well and yet not know it well enough to let it guide me every day?

My life is full of wonderful examples of how opportunities arose and I ventured forth, though fearfully, trusting the outcome to God. I wouldn't have written *Each Day a New Beginning* or any other book had I not been open to an opportunity that beckoned. I trembled many steps of the way then and still do. I do know deep in my heart that I'm never given more than I can handle, and I am given a variety of opportunities in order to fulfill the job God has planned for me. Anxiety leaves me when I remember this wise advice given to me so many years ago.

I'm on course. We're all on course. No matter how rocky it feels some days, all is well.

Our own well-being is enhanced each time
we put someone else's well-being first.
—*April 12*

I am struggling to be "okay" today. I woke up feeling isolated from my Higher Power and then tried to make my husband fill the void. He resisted and I got ugly and then, of course, had an amend to make. We're not fighting, but I'm still feeling edgy and, in all honesty, itching to fight some more.

I get so ashamed of this immaturity. For a few hours I discard everything the program has taught me. I get some perverse pleasure out of being nasty and punishing others. But beneath the veneer of pleasure, I'm feeling the pain of the isolation I create when I'm into my self-centeredness.

It's definitely a day when I should be reflecting on all the blessings in my life—family relationships, an understanding spouse with whom I share the program, wonderful friends, and work that brings me much pleasure. Instead, I've created a stumbling block with the focus I've placed on myself. I feel like such a novice today in regard to life and how this program works. I'm not looking with love toward others; I'm waiting for others to demonstrate my importance to them.

Being able to see what I'm doing is, at least, progress. Just sitting here writing about it is lessening my hatefulness. And yet I know that I must vigilantly look with love toward others, Acting As If, if necessary, to keep the return to hatefulness and isolation away.

How complicated I'm making life today. The sun is shining; the sky is brilliant blue; I'm sober and guaranteed God's unconditional love. Isn't that enough?

As we think, so we are.

—September 27

I was strongly influenced more than a decade ago by an article I read in *Psychology Today* on imaging and its power to change our lives. At the time I was fearfully contemplating my final oral exams, so I used the article as a tool in my personal life. Daily I imaged the exam experience, alway successfully answering the questions in a poised, articulate manner. I envisioned all of us smiling at one another throughout the two hours.

By the time the exam occurred, I felt confident and quite ready. I was no longer fearful. I felt as though I'd been through it successfully many times before. The actual exam experience mirrored my image of it, quite exactly. I was poised and articulate. We did smile a lot and I passed.

I'm reminded of my preparation for that experience frequently and have used imaging on many occasions since. It's been particularly helpful at work. I'm quite certain that my Higher Power is close at hand when I use imaging. In some instances, I've even felt that experiencing my Higher Power and this process are connected somehow at the most elementary level. Imaging is like prayer: it soothes and assures me that all is well, it changes my perspective by broadening my options, and it increases my awareness of my potential.

It's really unfortunate and even borders on insanity that I forget to use this powerful gift and instead give power to a negative use of imaging. We are just as capable of causing personal failure through believing ourselves incapable. My golf game is great evidence of that!

What we...achieve depends greatly on
what we believe about ourselves....

—*November 27*

I'm suffering with a cold today and feel quite child-like, wishing my mother could apply a mustard poultice and give me a vanilla ice cream Dixie cup and some ginger ale as she did when I was a child. I've blocked many of the loving exchanges between my mother and me from my mind, but I do recall, quite vividly, her tenderness when I was ill, lying on our living room couch. I'm grateful she and I share a very warm relationship now, but I was generally certain as a young girl that she disliked me—except when I was sick.

I find it hard now to slow down and nurture myself when I'm vulnerable and a bit sick. I force myself into activity that heightens my symptoms. And yet I do believe we can think ourselves into illness or into health. Thus, I struggle between ignoring my cold and sinus congestion, possibly spreading my germs to others, or giving in fully to my symptoms and feeling guilty because of my lack of productivity. Perhaps at the root of my struggle is this need to *always* be productive—always achieving—always striving toward the next goal. I hate reading articles or hearing discussions where others imply that the need to be productive is proportional to low self-esteem. I generally feel confident and self-assured. Not many days do I want to hide under the covers or my desk because of lagging self-esteem. And I value my productivity. True, it's hard for me to spend a whole evening watching TV, but I reject the notion, as an absolute, that my need to be productive comes out of feelings of worthlessness.

101

I can't comfortably ignore the creative urge within for long or I get depressed. Being productive releases it and my mood elevates. To me that's not evidence of low self-esteem. Or am I protesting too much?

*We have met certain people who inspired
laughter....*

—March 11

I don't have a sense of humor about politics, and that
causes stress and anger in my personal life during this
current political campaign. My spouse loves to poke
fun at the candidates. And I get angry when it's my
candidate he's attacking. I grew up in a family devoted
to one party, and I opted for the opposition. We fought
for years, which I'm sure is why I still react to my husband's attacks on my political party and candidate. I
take them personally, even though they aren't directed
at me. This has put a strain on our relationship for the
past month. I've constructed a wall between us that I
retreat behind every time he jabs my candidate. Then
I punish him with silence. Pretty silly behavior for a
woman with this much recovery under her belt.

I know that a sense of humor provides a healthy perspective on life. I've often had an experience turn
around 180 degrees after seeing the lighter side. My
spouse frequently reminds me to lighten up, but I get
mad because he's discounting my seriousness. I feel
pretty caught up in some crazy, overly serious thinking. I need to stand back and remember what a boss
told me half-a-dozen years ago: "It won't matter in fifty
years." In reality, of course, it won't matter in fifty
days. Whatever I was upset over two weeks ago, I've
forgotten.

I'm really so much happier when I'm lighthearted,
and I know I can make a choice to look on the bright,
humorous side. I don't like being around too serious,
humorless folks, yet I become this way myself, and then

I feel shame. I'm not powerless over my thoughts and behavior, but I certainly act as if I am, to no one's advantage.

Each of us tells a story with our lives....
—*December 6*

I once told a friend that after my death I hoped people would say I had lived a life of integrity and made the people in my life feel loved and special. What is painfully evident, on many days, is that I'm not living up to my own ideals. I'm not looking at all my associates with love. I neglect some special people in my life, and I'm not as full of integrity as I'd like. And yet I know I'm not a total failure!

What I have to do is keep reminding myself to show love, to listen attentively, to act according to my principles. I'm so grateful for the Twelve Steps because they help me remember my ideals, but I am ashamed that my natural instincts can't always assure admirable behavior.

In the same way that I must recall my Higher Power's image, I must remind myself to slow down and be thoughtful and loving in my actions toward others. Sometimes I try to see a Spirit Light in the people I'm working with. I sense a connection between us far more powerful than the conversation. I do believe that we are in each other's lives for the fulfillment of mutual purposes. It is not God's plan for us to be adversaries. My own ego creates any adversarial situation.

To look around with the loving eyes of a child shouldn't be work for me. After all these years, it should come naturally, shouldn't it?

Deciding day by day where we want to go
with our lives ushers in adventure....
—December 20

I'm not sure I'd say each day feels adventurous, but deciding for myself what I'm going to do and how I'll do it is empowering, and definitely was a new adventure some years back. Before recovery I passively "went along." I chose an occupation based on what others thought. I married when I shouldn't have because I couldn't say I'd changed my mind. I adopted the opinions of friends rather than defining my own values. All that began to change in my recovery and each day felt like an adventure. I "honeymooned" for many months.

Now I feel good making my own decisions. I never feel my fate rests in the hands of others—friends or strangers. I have a sense of excitement and health because I know my experiences will mirror my attitudes and my behavior. I can determine the kind of day I'll have and learn what I choose to learn.

When I look back on this day as it slips away, I see my experiences were just as ordered. The morning was smooth, filled with a positive, supportive atmosphere at work. The afternoon may have been more intense, but the tension was broken by lots of laughter. And this evening I got agitated because someone didn't agree with me, but I backed off, remembering the greater goal of sharing love, not just opinions.

I did determine, moment by moment, just what I'd experience. It's awesome to experience the breadth of the power of choice. It's humbling to accept the outcome when that choice is for "Thy will, not mine."

I will look for the signs of my benefactor today.

—*November 2*

I've been lacking in gratitude for the past few days, and this is not unusual for me. It's apparent I need to regularly recall all the good that has come my way and thank my Higher Power. I too easily take my health and happiness for granted, my comfortable home and good spouse, my rewarding job and loving family relationships. Stopping to think and look around me quite overwhelms me when I reflect on where my life was headed just fifteen years ago. I'm convinced that my Higher Power intervened or I'd not be alive and where I am today.

But I need to feel gratitude for other ways my Higher Power daily intervenes—when I look up just in time to avoid a collision while in heavy traffic; when I remember something important I'd forgotten; and, most importantly, when a loved one enters my circle of space just to say, "Hello, I'm here."

The signs of my Higher Power are everywhere—in the letters from home, the calls from friends, the smiles from my husband, the flowers on the coffee table, the ripples of laughter over a good story, the hug from a special person.

The thing I relearn every time I remember my blessings and become closer to my Higher Power is that my Higher Power really cares and really is present for me.

Whatever our pain, it is lessened by turning our attention elsewhere. . . .

—*February 11*

I'm quite struck by an awareness I had at a meeting today. Our topic was fear. I had awakened with a twinge of fear again today. As we shared, one by one, our personal struggles with fear, I was able to clearly see how I was contributing to my own fear. For sure my fears now are minimal compared to the fears of my childhood or throughout my twenties and thirties. But the reality is that I'd begun to give fear space in my life again.

Even more importantly, I realized that with the amount of time I've given to introspection these last few months, I've inadvertently increased my fear. It's not easy to articulate, really, but I do know that what we focus on looms larger in our lives.

I believe that *as we think, so we are.* These last few months, in my journaling, I've given much greater attention to my serious, darker side, than to my free-spirited side.

I certainly don't mean introspection isn't good for me. The Fourth Step is all about seeing myself as I really am. At the same time, I think I'm capable of causing a minor fear to spread like a virus by giving it more attention than I give my Higher Power. Thinking and talking and writing about my fears haven't eliminated them. Some of their power as secrets has been sapped by my openness about them, but still I've kept them too active with far too much attention.

Too much of anything is a sure way to get off track.

We are ready for whatever comes.

At a meeting tonight a woman shared how believing that a Universal Spiritual Force is in charge of her life keeps her sane and quiet in spite of the changes she's experiencing. Listening to her, I realized I've had very few major upheavals in the last four or five years and my belief in a Universal Spiritual Force has grown rusty. I guess I've gotten a bit complacent, spiritually. I still visit with God every day, and I do believe that care and protection are promised me and that I'm where I need to be to fulfill God's plan. But I sometimes keep my God thoughts so small and personal that I forget how vast the God-force really is.

It's comforting to dwell, once again, on a set of ideas that brought such longed-for peace to my life in my early years of sobriety. A personal relationship with God is necessary for me, but staying in touch, emotionally and mentally, with the Universal Spiritual Force adds an important element to my perspective. Just thinking about it now enhances both my belief that *all is well* and my trust that *we are* all *here by design fulfilling our unique destinies.*

Twelve Step meetings guarantee important new insights we need to continue to grow and change. I'm deeply touched at how many miracles have occurred in all our lives simply by sitting together and sharing honestly who we are and what we believe without fear of judgment or recrimination. How glad I am right now to be thinking of the Universal Spiritual Force; it offers me profound security. The meeting tonight dusted off this anchor, and I'm so grateful.

Perhaps we try to see too far ahead.
—*November 5*

I'm not at all sure how the change has come about, but I am dwelling more in the present than at any time before. In my earlier, sad and drunken years, I waited and waited for the tomorrow that promised to fulfill my fantasies of "happily ever after." Sobriety has come close to making that early fantasy a reality. But my real point is that I always used to project into the future where I hoped happiness awaited. I never clung to the moment at hand which, although pain-filled much of the time, was at least real and was offering me opportunities to make changes in my life. I declined.

Now I relish much more each day as it comes, because the older I get, the more quickly time seems to pass. I realize I may not have as many years left as I've already lived; I don't want to let them go by unnoticed. I look at family, friends, my spouse and treasure the time we have. If I focus on the thought that someday one of us will be gone, I am filled with dread. This reality makes living each passing moment so important.

I never could figure out the future anyway when I used to try so hard to control the outcome. Nothing about my life today is as I'd pictured it. The same is no doubt true of what will come next. Perhaps age has blessed me with at least enough wisdom to let the future take care of itself.

Today is enough to focus on. I believe it will offer me all that I need to do and know and I'll hear much more of God's message if I'm attuned to this moment. I'm sure I block out the messages I'm supposed to hear when my mind's on "then" rather than "now."

Behaving the way we honestly and sincerely believe God wants us to behave eliminates our confusion.

—November 6

I went to my nephew's baptism this morning. Among the minister's remarks was a recollection of his mother telling him when he was a youngster, "When you aren't sure what to do in a certain situation, do the right thing." The congregation laughed, yet I'm sure we all recognized her wisdom. There *is* always the right thing to do regardless of the circumstance. If I have doubt, I need only get quiet to discover the right thing. Many instances don't even require a moment of stillness; I instinctively know the proper choice to make.

I took an opportunity this morning to share with two friends my deep feelings of appreciation that they're in my life. I supported their strengths and the course each has charted for her life. It wasn't really a matter of me finding God's will in the situation as much as choosing to openly affirm another's identity and existence, rather than keeping my thoughts quiet. And the real reward, of course, in expressing such thoughts is that I felt as good in the sharing as each of them did in the listening.

My well-being is enhanced each opportunity I take to openly show love to another person. I do believe it's God's hope that we'll make the choice, the right choice, to affirm those who are in our lives. I'm coming to believe that's our only "job" of importance in this life. My self-love inches up a notch each time I genuinely feel and then tell another of my love for him or her. It simplifies living when I focus on loving.

There are many victories in our future....
　　　　　　　　　　　　　　　—November 7

My definition of *victory* has changed, perhaps one would say matured, with age. Victory used to mean winning rather than losing, whether in a game of tennis or an argument. It was overcoming an adversary or at least an adversarial situation. Much of my self-esteem was measured in terms of those victories.

A victory now is when I make a healthy choice for myself. It's choosing to act with respect and love in situations that nettle me or ones I'd rather have avoided altogether. It's putting another's interests or needs before my own. It's letting go of outcomes and trusting them to God. It's surrendering in an argument.

The principles of any Twelve Step program promise me abundant victories providing I keep the Steps manifest in my life. How easy my future looks when anticipated from this vantage point. I'm guaranteed happiness, joy and laughter, personal serenity, and God's blessing so long as I fulfill my part of the contract—which is to Let Go and Let God.

I'm overwhelmed with gratitude right now because of all the victories I'm experiencing as a result of surrendering. Knowing my future will be as rewarding and as fulfilling as my ability to sway with the changing life currents takes away these latent anxieties.

I looked around the dinner table today at family and friends and felt blessed. How did I get here, in this loving setting, except for this program? And this can and will be my home for as long as I think of victory in terms of surrender rather than someone else's defeat. This makes possible a long road of happiness ahead.

We can reflect on what's gone before, and trust that which faces us now.

I'm quite mellow presently. I recall vividly those years when I wasn't. I couldn't even have defined it—at least not from my own experience. What's different now? Is my life easy and manageable? Are all my problems solved? I think not, really. A better assessment is that I rely more now on my Higher Power. Most days, I don't doubt that God is in charge and that God's will is supreme.

I tried to believe both of these truths for many years and did believe them intellectually. I simply couldn't act accordingly. One minute I'd say, "God is in charge," and then I'd assert my own will. I do still act willfully but not as often. The change in me seems mystical at times. It came about almost imperceptibly. I actually find myself passing up chances to get upset. Very few situations seem worth turmoil. In my youth and even into my early recovery, I turned most circumstances into traumas, finding comfort in crisis. I didn't believe it would ever be different. When it began to change, I tried to recapture the spirit of crisis. My life felt boring without emotional upheaval. And now it feels restful, and I treasure the quiet spaces that I know will be my constant companions as long as I let God's will be my guide.

113

We are just where we need to be today.
—*November 9*

This thought is probably one of the most comforting gifts this program has given me. In the early years it offered me peace when I was considering suicide. It made it possible for me to believe that every circumstance, grave or terrifying, was designed for my personal growth and ultimate well-being. It allowed me to relax, believing "this too shall pass." It continues to help me absorb people's barbs and the tension or turmoil that plagues me. I know now that I've chosen my route in this life and that God is forever helping me move in the right direction.

I've talked with a number of friends lately about the idea that we write our own "scripts" in this life. I was first introduced to this idea a dozen or more years ago, and I've always been intrigued by it and more or less inclined to believe it. I do think mental and spiritual health require I take total responsibility for my actions and attitude. So to believe my intentions were developed even before I lived them, feels not farfetched but rather quite logical.

And this, too, brings another measure of comfort. I'm not only where I need to be, I'm where I decided I must be to gain all that God has intended I should gain in this life. This means no more blame on parents or past lovers or present circumstances. I'm in charge of where I'm going and where I've been. It's an empowering idea and one that fills me with awe and a strong sense of spiritual well-being.

I believe I'm on course—the course God and I have chosen—and all is well. This isn't as easy to believe every day as it is today, but years of experiencing circumstances working out in beneficial ways makes belief much easier with each passing struggle.

We can decide to let go of a situation that we can't control. . . .

It's crazy how I sometimes slip and try to control situations that are clearly beyond my powers and, quite frankly, none of my business. I sometimes wonder about myself. How long do I have to live with Step One before I fully internalize that I'm powerless over *everything* and *everybody* but myself?

This past week I placed my attention on a friend's eating habits, at first cajoling, then giving unwanted feedback, and finally shaming him with criticism. I was promptly told to go to Al-Anon. Though I already do, weekly, at times like this it seems to no avail. The desire to control others is so subtle and so insidious. In a matter as simple as "suggesting" someone not overeat or lay off the candy, it's all too easy to deny that I'm trying to control someone else's behavior. Outwardly I say I'm only being a loving friend. What's my motivation? What do I care, really?

And the fact is—I don't actually care. Controlling others, or at least the attempt to do so, becomes habitual. *Not* trying to control them can only become a habit with hard work and regular practice. I really wouldn't think of trying to control an active alcoholic's drinking anymore. Nor would I try to control traffic jams or the weather. But there are situations that seduce me, and avoiding the seduction is no different than letting God be in charge of sunrises.

116

The solution to any problem lies within it.
                              —December 22

Problems come in such varied sizes and shapes. Some only affect me emotionally. Others stir my whole being—I become physically and emotionally distressed. Fortunately, most of my problems are merely irritants, but whatever the problem, I keep having to relearn that any one of them is only as troubling as I make it! I can blow it away, laugh it off, or obsess over it and make it bigger.

Turning to my Higher Power is the only sure way of letting a problem resolve itself. As if by magic, when I turn to spiritual thoughts—perhaps picturing my Higher Power coming to my rescue—my breathing slows and deepens and my shoulders relax. I feel peace from deep within, and my perspective changes dramatically. Frankly, I have to work hard to keep a problem a problem for long since I found this program for living. When I practice these principles in all my affairs, it's pretty difficult to stay stuck on a problem for long.

It's so frighteningly easy for me to imagine and cultivate a problem at times, one would think I actually enjoy creating crises. The only good that I can possibly attach to this situation is that it ultimately pushes me toward my Higher Power. Sometimes, though, I drag my feet rather than hurry.

We must learn how to act rather than react.
—*February 8*

How easily I can overreact when somebody meddles in my affairs! I was having a productive day—slow, yet meaningful. I was comfortably attentive to all my affairs and able to pause, when necessary, to sort through my thoughts before taking action or responding to a situation. That is, up until I found that an associate had stuck her nose into one of my projects, causing turmoil for everyone involved.

In a flash, all my serenity was gone. No more quiet pauses! I was on the attack. I accept that my craziness is because I don't trust her. She is an incessant controller whom I can't control!

Woe is me. And not three hours prior to getting news of her meddling, I told my AA group that I was having great success in seeing others as spiritually connected to me rather than separate. I had waxed eloquent about how this had helped me to see situations less adversarially. I went on to say my adherence to this idea had softened my brittle edges considerably and made all my experiences, both at work and at home, far more joy-filled.

And in an instant, I threw it all out the window. It's ironic that at that same meeting our discussion topic was Step Six. I sat there comfortably believing I had been entirely ready to have God remove my obsession to pass judgment on others. What a quick lesson I got!

We need to befriend all of our emotions.
—*November 10*

I don't like some of my emotions, and my inability to befriend them makes them loom more awful in my mind. It's crazy but I get angry at my anger. I don't like letting something get the best of me, and that's how I feel when I've just had a bout with anger. I feel shame that I can't just let go of it but, instead, let it control me. I always beat myself up, for a bit at least, before I remember that I'm human, not perfect, and my emotions can't control me unless I relinquish control over both my attitude and my behavior.

Being consumed by an emotion that has run amuck is too easy sometimes, particularly if I'm tired or hungry or not feeling well. But if I'm feeling good, getting regular exercise, finding time for my visits with God, the emotion that most often colors my journey is quiet joy. And that emotion I befriend easily.

A sponsor once told me that all emotions must be my friends for me to understand and accept myself. I readily believe that intellectually. But in practice I often withdraw. When I do, I punish myself and the people around me. When I'm feeling less acceptable emotions, such as anger, depression, or jealousy, I do know that practicing a positive emotion, Acting As If, if necessary, can guide me to a better state of mind. In the short run, this feels great. In the long run, all my emotions are faces of me—each deserves equal time, attention, and love to minimize its long-term negative effects.

I really feel more mellow than I sound here. I find it curious that I've made a bigger issue of my difficulty with emotions than is really the case, I think.

119

Our minds mold who we become.

I realize I'm still in the process of becoming. I've grown beyond the always-terrified child, and I'm growing beyond the always insecure, self-conscious woman. Through the tools of sobriety, prayer, imagery, self-disclosure, forgiveness, and the practice of love, I'm developing into a woman I like being with and one I'm not very often ashamed of or embarrassed about.

Accepting responsibility for who I was in the past, who I am every moment of the present, and who I'll be for all of my tomorrows fills me with awe. It is exhilarating. For decades I blamed my family's politics and my first husband's alcoholism and philandering for my anger, fears, and insecurities. My growth was stunted, and it wasn't until I found recovery that I learned to act on rather than react to all the circumstances troubling me. What a gift this has been! It's still one that I need to unwrap every day, or I'll slip back into blaming others for my thoughts and my behavior.

I've changed in significant ways, I think, and yet my first impulse is often to respond like my old reactive self. I must be vigilant. My recent outburst over a co-worker's meddling is not the behavior I'm trying to mold in myself. But I'm the only one who can make certain I'll not revert to the old behavior.

How far we have come!

It's good for my soul and my continued growth to recount for myself and others, too, the details of "what it was like, what happened, and what it's like now." I was on a suicide course, doing "street" drugs, "street" men, and excessive alcohol. My mind often didn't track; I collected speeding tickets like souvenirs, and I seldom knew the names of my many intimate partners.

How I escaped that life seems no less than a miracle. I've come to know years of solid recovery and clearheadedness. I have real friends, a loving marriage, and a family that looks forward to my visits. And, I have my writing, truly a gift from my Higher Power.

I sit here today in my big old recliner and marvel at the changes in these few short years. I was so certain fifteen years ago I knew where my life was going, but my destination so far doesn't at all match my predictions. Thanks to my Higher Power! My earlier direction promised few achievements and no secure relationships. The real joy in recalling how far I've come is that I know my future can be filled with exciting possibilities too. What I do with my opportunities is up to me, but sobriety at least makes possible choices that are well thought out and true to my needs. I have faith that at some future date, I'll be able to recall fondly how far I've come, provided that sobriety remains my number one priority.

Feeling inferior can become a habit.

—*July 10*

Some days I can move very quickly from a feeling of confidence and joy to twinges of fear that I'm not measuring up. I just had one of those experiences. I had breakfast with a few friends, and we laughed and talked. I felt loved and loving, and then I came home and my spouse suggested we invite some folks over who he thinks are great conversationalists and bundles of fun. I immediately felt I was neither! Those feelings come, at least in part, from my old childhood fears of not measuring up. But I wasn't expecting to feel those feelings today.

I've *never* actually heard that I'm boring, nor have people indicated they'd rather not talk to me. And yet I assume both sometimes. I'm not surprised that I feel that way when I'm depressed. But today I was feeling content with myself, or so I thought, and wham—I got it between the eyes.

Perhaps I'll always struggle with my self-esteem, and I guess that's okay. It helps me to understand the many others who struggle with these same issues.

The gratitude I feel right now, though, that I can talk over my feelings with my spouse, getting affirmation from him that I'm really an interesting and fun woman, is the program's best gift.

My feelings just an hour ago are a good reminder that every time I focus on me and how I'm doing rather than showing and feeling appreciation for others, I'm headed for trouble. My ego is all too ready to accommodate craziness, and I don't have to succumb, ever.

Our loving thoughts for persons close and far away always reach their destination.
—July 11

I seem to feel so much better, more content, and closer to my Higher Power on days I take time to quietly send loving thoughts to my family and friends, thinking of each, one by one. Some days it feels like a mindless ritual, and yet I do it. They don't seem so distant anymore, even though some of us are thousands of miles apart. My love for them has grown in this prayerful process, and this is the best gift of all.

A sponsor told me years ago to pray for my first husband. It was hard because I was filled with such rage. I struggled at first, but the real surprise was how much my prayer changed my attitude, not just about him, but about me too. I think that's what sending loving thoughts to others is really about.

Thoughts have substance and have an effect on the lives of others, but I believe that the real gifts eventually return to me. I become more accepting of others when I practice the art of thinking and sending love to those who are *of* my life, though maybe not *in* my life every day. My love for myself grows in proportion to my love for others, but I have always found it hard to love myself when I didn't like others. I'd hear people say I needed to love myself if I was ever to really love others. I didn't understand it then. I still don't. What has worked for me, though, is to send love outward, and little by little I'm feeling more loving inside. I may not be doing it "right," but I like how my way makes me feel.

Loving thoughts can and will keep me sane. My job is just to remember to think them.

Epilogue

When I realized my journal would be published, it came to me that I was doing a *very* public Fourth and Fifth Step. In many entries, my character defects reared their ugly heads. And with regularity my own struggle with letting God be in charge of my life and the outcomes right for me was starkly apparent. I worried that you, my friends and readers, would think less of me since you'd be privy to the *real* me. All my life I've struggled with wanting people to see me as I *wanted* to be, not as I really was. And here, over these months of journaling, I was revealing *all* of me, the ugliness along with the beauty.

Judy, my friend and editor, asked me about this. She wanted me to be sure I would remain comfortable going public with the details of those parts of myself that I don't relish. I thought long and hard about it. I prayed about it and concluded that I'd risk whatever the outcome to my self-disclosures. In my day-to-day personal life, I've believed, firmly, that keeping secrets harms our growth, our recovery, and it definitely harms our relationships.

My hope, here, has been to further strengthen my relationship with all of you. I knew that honesty about who I really am, not who I only wish I were, is the only pathway to a deepened relationship.

Believe me, I've "let it all hang out." In rereading these entries, I wanted to make myself sound more loving, less self-centered, more *recovered*. I felt embarrassed, at times ashamed, and very humbled by this confrontation with myself. I clearly see the distance I've yet to go, but I also see how far I've come. And that's even more important. One of the values of any Fourth and Fifth Step is that we can and should gauge the progress we've made. We too often forget this is a program promoting Progress, Not Perfection. Just as I'm publicly disclosing my continuing struggles on these pages, I want to publicly pat myself on the back, as I think we all should, for continuing to work on recovery and personal growth One Day at a Time. My Higher Power is not expecting perfection of me. Only I do that. And I am making strides in accepting my own humanity, I *think*.

I want to thank you for sharing my journey. I hope the experience has been helpful to you. I hope you have gained some clarity regarding your own struggles and progress. I hope you have been moved to journal a bit, but even more I hope you have been moved to nurture that small child within. She's the one who is struggling to live up to the principles that you want guiding your life.

I've made many references to my own principles, particularly in the introduction. Most of them are implied within my journal entries, but it's helpful for me to be specific about them, on a day-to-day basis, so I offer them here. They are my measuring stick, and some days I measure up better than others. How well you know!

1. Along the way I've expanded my understanding of "the program" only to discover that it will always invite yet a deeper level of commitment and understanding.
2. I've praised my attempts to live more in the here and now. The present is all there is—and yet I must

be vigilant about my adherence to this principle. It's all too easy to lose my focus.

3. The past has no reality, no power over me except what I choose to give it. My thoughts, noisy and troubled or quiet and serene, are in my charge.

4. I believe my soul is on a journey, one made by choice. My stops along the way to my destination are not happenstance but rather are assuring me of the growth that is mine to experience.

5. Each of us is unique and needed by those who are sharing our journey.

6. We're each blessed with talents that only await our recognition and celebration.

7. I've learned that exercise and good nutrition offer a daily boost to my self-esteem.

8. Following through on projects, disciplining myself to continue persevering, strengthens my evolving, healthy sense of self.

9. Slowing down to appreciate the moment's voice or view or dream enhances my serenity and thus my well-being.

10. Listening intently to another's words promises me a connection to my Higher Power.

11. Any expression of gratitude gives me additional blessings in return.

12. Acknowledging God's presence in every situation, within every person I encounter, extinguishes my fear.

13. Drawing within myself to get centered prepares me fully for the moment, the encounter. All tension leaves when I breathe in the strength promised by my Higher Power.

14. When I'm acting from a posture of love, I have no fear and relationship ripples become smooth.

15. Each person's perspective is valid and need not be defended or attacked.
16. A quiet mind knows no fear, realizes all knowledge, and moves ahead with confidence and ease.

Until we meet again...keep going to meetings; keep talking to friends; stay hopeful. *We are* on the mend.

Postscript

Dear Readers,

It has been a couple of months since I said to Judy, my editor, "I'm done." How surprised I am that I now feel compelled to have one more say.

I've just returned from another business trip and I'm at peace. I was joyful and peaceful throughout the trip. Unlike my trip many months ago when I wrote about my despair and loneliness for my "space" here in my comforting study, on this trip each *space* I entered comforted me. Once again I'm reminded how everything changes; nothing stays the same. I'm continuing to grow, and my sense of security and well-being grows too. They also recede, on occasion, like the ocean tides, but for now they are expanding.

I'm quite certain that my own joyful attitude and my decision to stay in the present throughout my trip kept me comfortable and spirit-filled. It's really so simple. The program suggests—and sponsors sometimes admonish us—to live One Day at a Time. And yet, at times, with relish even, I jump to months and years from now and get crippled with fear.

But the power to stop negative thoughts is mine. And the decision to live only *here and now* wherever here and now is, is likewise in my power. I exercised it well on this trip.

I just wanted to share with you one last experience before bringing the final closure to our "conversation." I am buoyed up, profoundly so once again, by how committed my Higher Power is to making my life peaceful. All I have to do is trust and know eventually everytime, everywhere, that all will be well.

I know me well enough that I'll learn this again and again over the years. But my joy today is worth sharing with friends. I leave you now.

Go peacefully, today.

THE AUTHOR